I0814124

CLIPP 45

College Library Information on Policy and Practice

from the College Libraries Section of the Association of College and Research Libraries

Open Educational Resources

COMPILED AND WRITTEN BY MARY FRANCIS

Association of College and Research Libraries
A division of the American Library Association
Chicago, Illinois 2021

The paper used in this publication meets the minimum requirements of American National Standard for Information Sciences–Permanence of Paper for Printed Library Materials, ANSI Z39.48-1992. ∞

Library of Congress Control Number: 2021931261

Copyright ©2021 by the Association of College and Research Libraries. All rights reserved except those which may be granted by Sections 107 and 108 of the Copyright Revision Act of 1976.
Printed in the United States of America.

25 24 23 22 21 5 4 3 2 1

TABLE OF CONTENTS

CLS CLIPP COMMITTEE

Luann DeGreve
Benedictine University
Lisle, Illinois

Jessica Brangiel
Swarthmore College
Swarthmore, Pennsylvania

Sara Metz
Lone Star College—Atascocita Center
Houston, TX 7

Patricia Jean Mileham
Valparaiso University
Valparaiso, Indiana

INTRODUCTION

The College Library Information on Policy and Practice (CLIPP) publishing program, under the auspices of the College Libraries Section of the Association of College and Research Libraries, provides college and small university libraries analysis and examples of library practices and procedures. This CLIPP provides information on Open Educational Resources. Open Educational Resources (OER) were first discussed in 2002 at a United Nations Educational, Scientific and Cultural Organization (UNESCO) forum which was intended "to develop together a universal educational resource available for the whole of humanity" (2002). They were seen as a method to improve global education by ensuring access to high-quality course materials. Since that time, there have been a variety of initiatives at various levels to implement OER. We are now at a point where the work of the early adopters can be consolidated to provide insights for those looking to provide OER.

While there are case studies that provide insight on how individual institutions have implemented OER initiatives, there is no overview study that provides a context for such initiatives within the larger college population. This CLIPP allows librarians to survey what is being done on a larger scale whether they already are a part of an OER initiative, are looking to form such an initiative, or are unfamiliar with such initiatives.

The survey first gathers information on OER or other affordable course content initiatives that are occurring at college libraries. These questions look at items such as funding of the initiative. These structural questions provide libraries considering OER with ideas on how to implement such a program on their own campuses. The survey then looks specifically at what actions libraries are taking to support OER. Given the range of possible activities, it is helpful to see what other libraries are doing and to consider how the library may expand by offering additional services. The survey finally asks for comments from respondents as to the future of libraries and OER. These comments can help vocalize the need for such initiatives. The final section of this CLIPP provides a selection of documents related to OER initiatives as examples.

LITERATURE REVIEW AND BIBLIOGRAPHY

History of OER

This CLIPP looks at how libraries are taking part in college initiatives related to Open Educational Resources (OER). UNESCO defines OERs as "teaching, learning and research materials in any medium—digital or otherwise—that reside in the public domain or have been released under an open license that permits no-cost access, use, adaptation and redistribution by others with no or limited restrictions" (2019). These educational materials take many forms: textbooks, videos, homework assignments, lecture notes, simulations, lesson plans, worksheets, test banks, etc.

Smith and Casserly (2006) note, "At the heart of the open educational resources movement is the simple and powerful idea that the world's knowledge is a public good and that technology in general and the World Wide Web in particular provide an extraordinary opportunity for everyone to share, use, and reuse that knowledge." Walz notes that OER builds on the ideas of three other movements:

> The Open Access movement, which provides digital, online and no-cost access to literature and increasingly to repositories, data and other resources; the Distance Education movement, which adopts communications technology and instructional design for learning; and the Open Source movement in which computer code developers share, modify, and redistribute software code under an open license (2015).

One of the important characteristics of OER is the fact that they are open licensed. This means that they are freely accessible as well as being open to adaptation and alteration. This differs from items that are simply open access where the work cannot be altered in any way. Wiley lays out the ways in which OER can be used as retain, revise, remix, redistribute, and reuse (n.d.). Many open-licensed materials use Creative Commons licensing in order to clarify what can be done with the work. Creative Commons offers six main licenses under which to publish which are formed from the combination of four features. From the least to most restrictive they are attribution; share alike; noncommercial; no derivatives; noncommercial and share alike; and noncommercial, share alike, and no derivatives. Creative Commons describes these licenses.

> **Attribution (BY)**
> All CC licenses require that others who use your work in any way must give you credit the way you request but not in a way that suggests you endorse them or their use. If they want to use your work without giving you credit or for endorsement purposes, they must get your permission first.

ShareAlike (SA)
You let others copy, distribute, display, perform, and modify your work as long as they distribute any modified work on the same terms. If they want to distribute modified works under other terms, they must get your permission first.

NonCommercial (NC)
You let others copy, distribute, display, perform, and (unless you have chosen No Derivatives) modify and use your work for any purpose other than commercially unless they get your permission first.

NoDerivatives (ND)
You let others copy, distribute, display, and perform only original copies of your work. If they want to modify your work, they must get your permission first (2019).

Textbook Costs

The development of OER within higher education has often been discussed as a means to address issues related to increasing textbook prices. Numerous studies have looked at the costs of textbooks with Popken (2015) finding that textbook prices have risen 1,041 percent between 1977 and 2015. This is three times the rate of inflation between 2002 and 2012 (GAO, 2013). The College Board notes the average estimate for books and supplies is $1,298 per year.

Unlike tuition and room and board, textbook costs are an expense over which students have some autonomy. So, when dealing with limited funds, students can simply not purchase the textbooks for their courses. This decision, however, can affect grades and ultimately retention and graduation rates (Donaldson & Nelson 2012 in Goddsett, Loomis). Textbooks are used for learning new material, completing assignments, and studying for exams. "While increased access to textbooks alone will not ensure the success of college students, textbooks are generally recognized as being important learning resources" (Hilton, 2016).

These increases in price have resulted in students not taking specific courses (Okamoto, 2013). Almost 50 percent of students surveyed noted the cost of textbooks impacted how many or which classes they took (Senack, 2014). The Florida Virtual Campus reported that 47.6 percent of students occasionally or frequently take fewer courses and 45.5 percent of students do not register for a course due to the cost of the textbooks (2016).

If students do take a course, they do not necessarily purchase the textbook. Senack's report looked at responses from 2,039 students from 150 different campuses. He found that 65 percent of students had decided not to buy a textbook because it was too expensive, and of those students, 94 percent of them were concerned that not buying the textbook would hurt their grade. This is a concern in that "students are not only choosing *not* to purchase the materials they are assigned by their professor, but they are *knowingly* accepting the risk of a lower grade to avoid paying for the textbook" (2014). These numbers are similar to a 2016 survey conducted of more than 22,000 students from Florida institutions of higher education. It found that 66.6 percent of students did not purchase the required textbook due to cost (Florida Virtual Campus).

Not having the textbook can result in various outcomes, including dropping a course (26.1 percent of students in the Florida survey), withdrawing from a course (20.7 percent of students in the Florida survey), earning a poor grade (37.6 percent of students in the Florida survey), and failing a course (19.8 percent of students in the Florida survey).

Another finding of note in the Florida Virtual Campus survey was that the costs of textbooks were higher for students at colleges compared to universities. Costs were also higher for those seeking an associate or bachelor's degree compared to those seeking a master's or doctorate degree. These differences not only were found in the costs of textbooks. "Compared to university students, college students are more likely to take fewer courses, not register for a specific course, drop a course, or withdraw from a course due to the cost of textbooks" (Florida Virtual Campus, 2016). The Florida Virtual Campus survey has been completed twice in 2012 and 2016. While there are shifts within 1–2 percentage points, the responses have remained similar over the years.

In looking at the cost of textbooks, OER operates under the belief "that cost is a barrier to learning and to reduce that barrier, materials should be made freely available to learners and researchers in order to promote and democratize knowledge and learning" (Elliott & Fabbro, 2015). It is felt that by offering free course materials students will be spared the extra cost.

While there is no official number of the student cost savings through the use of OER, different groups have provided estimates. Achieving the Dream estimated that in the first two years of their grant program, students within the 2,946 classes offering OER saved an estimated $7.2 to $12.3 million. On average, a student in the initiative saved between $66 and $121 per course.

Faculty/Student Opinion of OER

The choice of required course materials ultimately rests with the faculty offering the course. It is therefore important to understand faculty opinions of OER. The first effort in the implementation of OER is faculty awareness and understanding of OER. In a 2014 survey of faculty members across the country, it was found that only 34 percent of the respondents had an awareness of OER. However, a more recent study by the Babson Group (Seaman, 2018) found that 46 percent of the 4,000 faculty members surveyed had an awareness of OER. This increase in awareness is the first step in increasing the use of OER.

The next step taken in the implementation of OER is discovering how faculty members select the materials they assign for their courses. Bell's survey on OER looked at faculty, their courses, and institutions in order to get specific information on their instructional content, where they discover it, and how they select it. His survey of approximately 1,400 faculty found that quality is the most important reason faculty select course materials followed by cost. While "personal reflection" is the primary reason faculty will implement OER, they do rely on peers and OER repositories to find materials. Librarians are not often identified as a resource for OER. His white paper concludes that "there remains much work to increase the number of faculty who adopt OER, and emphasizes the need for a discovery and evaluation tool that offers time saving ease of use for faculty searching for OER" (2018).

Faculty are motivated to implement OER for a number of reasons, including altruistic, commercial, and transformational incentives (Anderson et al., 2017). In campus visits with faculty, Griffiths et al. had faculty note that OER materials were more diverse, dynamic, interactive, contemporary, and relevant than traditional textbooks. This was due to the fact that when they moved beyond just a single textbook, faculty were likely to include a range of materials. Also, rather than sticking with one textbook over several years, faculty using OER included newer items. Plus, once they implemented OER, they saw increased student engagement with the materials. This engagement stems from the idea that often when faculty implement OER, they are focusing more on the needs of the students. This student-first attitude is often part of a larger pedagogical shift (2018).

Some of the barriers to implementing OER include concerns with copyright, quality, sustainability, interoperability, technical demands, cultural and language barriers, cost, exploitation of labor, and lack of institutional policies and incentives (Anderson et al., 2017). Some of these barriers can be met with further education—for example, increased understanding of copyright issues and technical considerations. Others need to be discussions on the quality of the material. Faculty have also noted "concerns over lack of familiarity with OER, availability of OER, and the additional time and effort required to use them, while administrators consider the overall business model required to support and sustain them over time" (Colson, Scott, & Donaldson, 2017). Some of the reasons faculty are not using OER are more basic, including lack of information about OER, lack of discoverability of repositories of OER, and confusion over the difference between OER and digital resources (Colson, 2017). Some faculty may also avoid the work of developing and publishing their own OER materials due to a promotion and tenure process that does not recognize OER.

There have also been studies done looking at how OER are perceived by those who use them. Hilton's survey of nine studies gathered data from 4,510 students and faculty. Overall, the perceived quality of the OER was similar to or higher than traditional textbooks. Students also held a higher opinion of OER due to the cost savings associated with their use (2016).

A wider look at the perception of OER can be seen in the report put out by Achieving the Dream. This group is made up of OER initiatives from thirty-eight community colleges from across the US. Within their 2018 report, they found that students find OER more relevant, easier to navigate, and better aligned with learning objectives than traditional textbooks.

Effectiveness of OER on Learning

In addition to the monetary benefit to students, OER is also promoted as a way for faculty members to have greater control of the content they provide to their students. Rather than relying on a commercial textbook, faculty can customize their materials to their specific courses. This can result in higher educational outcomes. These outcomes vary based on the students and the intent of the faculty members. In looking at case studies of OER use, some of the benefits noted by faculty who had implemented OER include "advance curricula, engage students in the creation of materials across a range of skill levels, and support students who frequently miss class" (Anderson et al., 2017).

Hilton maintains an updated annotated bibliography of research studies on OER at openedgroup.org. In his 2016 published literature review, he found that "in synthesizing these nine OER efficacy studies, an emerging finding is that utilizing OER does not appear to decrease student learning" (Hilton). While some may wish for a stronger positive connection between the use of OER and student learning, these findings may actually be the best possible. It is not expected that a simple change in the textbook will greatly impact student learning, so the move to an OER would also not provide such a result. However, for those concerned with the quality of OER materials, these studies show that there is no decrease in learning that supports the quality of the resources.

OER use also means that students will have immediate access to their course materials from the start of the class. While it is still early in their grant process, the Achieve to Dream initiative does expect to see a decreased time to graduate given the fact that students will not drop or avoid enrolling in specific courses due to the cost of the textbook (2018). Achieve the Dream is a network of 277 institutions dedicated to enhancing the success of students by improving education and enhancing equity. Their mission states their purpose is "to lead and support a national network of community colleges to achieve sustainable institutional transformation through sharing knowledge, innovative solutions and effective practices and policies leading to improved outcomes for all students."

Library Integration of OER

There have been a number of articles calling on librarians to take an active leadership role in the development of OER on their individual campuses (Bell, 2015; Jensen & West, 2015; Mitchell & Chu, 2014; Okamoto, 2013; Pitcher, 2014; Sutton & Chadwell, 2014; Anderson, Gaines, Leachman, & Williamson, 2017). ACRL has also noted the importance of OER through the development of a new OER and Affordability Roadshow. The tenets, experiences, and knowledge of librarians correspond to the ideal and implementation of OER. First, librarians believe in free access to information. They also have experience finding information which is necessary when helping faculty find OER that have already been created. Librarians also have experience organizing information that comes into play when OER materials must be put online for use by students. Librarians have established collaborative relationships with faculty. Librarians also have knowledge of copyright issues that arise when using and creating new materials. "Library expertise in copyright and licensing, networks of faculty relationships, and emerging involvement in instructional design and digital publishing present opportunities to create open education and affordability initiatives that will bear a lasting institution-wide contribution to student academic achievement and faculty engagement" (Walz, Jensen, & Salem, 2016, 9). Braddlee and VanScoy (2019) found in their survey of faculty members that they value librarians serving in traditional roles within OER initiatives.

Okamoto (2013) provides broad categorizations to the work libraries are doing in regard to OER initiatives, including advocacy, promotion, and discovery; evaluation, collection, preservation, and access; curation, creation, and facilitation; and funding. Smith and Lee (2017) provide a clear list of roles held by librarians within OER, including

- using outreach skills to advocate and promote OER;

- providing strategies to find and evaluate current, relevant, and high-quality OER;
- maintaining subject-based guides to find resources;
- providing long-term stable access to OER via institutional repositories;
- leveraging metadata, indexing, and classification skills to enhance access;
- adapting copyright expertise to help manage intellectual property rights and promote open licensing; and
- facilitating the curation and creation of OER.

Currently, there are a number of large initiatives on OER occurring at community colleges and large universities. The Community College Consortium for Open Educational Resources has formed out of the goal of managing the costs for their students. Achieving the Dream's OER initiative is "designed to help remove financial roadblocks that can derail students' progress and to spur other changes in teaching and learning and course design that will increase the likelihood of degree and certificate completion" (2016). Nagar and Hallam-Miller (2019) provide an overview of OER for libraries who are considering OER.

Large universities have the personnel and resources to undertake such initiatives. While these large initiatives do great work, there is less in the literature about the work being done by smaller programs on individual campuses. This survey will explore what college libraries are doing regarding OER and similar initiatives meant to provide low- to no-cost course materials for students. Parts of this survey were influenced by a 2016 survey on OER that was done by members of the Association of Research Libraries (ARL) and an international study performed by Bueno-de-la-Fuente, Robertson, and Boon in 2012.

In 2016, there was a survey of the Association of Research Libraries (ARL) to "determine the degree to which ARL member institutions are engaged in ACC [affordable course content] /OER advocacy, support, and development" (2). This survey gathered information from 65 out of the 124 ARL member libraries looking at the implementation, governance, funding, faculty incentive programs, policies and practices, support services and educational efforts, faculty engagement, library staffing, librarian knowledge, skills, and abilities, and librarian opinions of OER. The survey also gathered documents from member institutions.

Bueno-de-la-Fuente, Robertson, and Boon (2012) provided a look at how libraries are taking part in OER initiatives internationally. They found the main areas of library involvement dealt with description and classification, management, preservation, dissemination, and promotion of OER. They felt that it was important to promote the role that librarians can play in OER through their expertise and competencies.

While OER can benefit students both financially and educationally, it must be noted that OER in and of itself is not to be taken as the solution to the problems facing higher education. Crissinger (2015) describes how libraries must approach and advocate for OER realistically as one part of a shift in how faculty approach their courses and students by adapting innovative teaching practices.

OER Repositories

Due to the varied repositories and types, there can be some challenges for libraries that are looking to provide finding guides for already-produced OER. There are a number of repositories for OER content, including the following:

- BCcampus—A Canadian-based group providing access to open textbooks and information on how to create an open textbook. https://open.bccampus.ca/browse-our-collection/find-open-textbooks
- California Open Online Network for Education (Cool4Ed)—A group of three State of California Higher Education Systems providing access to textbooks and other course materials. Also highlighted are showcases describing how faculty have implemented OER. http://cool4ed.org
- Commonwealth of Learning OAsis—OAsis is the Commonwealth of Learning's (COL) online institutional repository for learning resources and publications. COL is an intergovernmental organization hosted by the Canadian government to promote the development and sharing of open learning and distance education knowledge, resources, and technologies. http://oasis.col.org
- Coursera—Coursera partners with universities and organizations to offer courses online. https://www.coursera.org
- Curriki—An educational nonprofit that provides access to K-12 class materials and a community to share and develop tools. https://www.curriki.org
- FlatWorld Knowledge—FlatWorld publishes textbooks and offers them at a reduced price. https://catalog.flatworldknowledge.com
- HathiTrust—A partnership of academic and research institutions offering a collection of millions of titles digitized from libraries around the world. https://www.hathitrust.org
- Lyryx Learning—Lyryx provides free textbooks in mathematics, economics, and business. It also provides customizable online homework products that can be used with the textbooks for a fee. https://lyryx.com
- Multimedia Educational Resource for Learning and Online Teaching (MERLOT)—MERLOT provides access to curated online learning and support materials and content creation tools. https://www.merlot.org/merlot
- North Carolina Learning Object Repository (NCLOR)—NCLOR collects documents, audio/video clips, simulations, learning modules, assessments, and more for K-12 teachers in North Carolina. https://explorethelor.org
- OER Commons—OER Commons is a public digital library of open educational resources. It contains materials for preschool-12 and higher education. Open Author also helps build Open Educational Resources, lesson plans, and courses. https://www.oercommons.org
- Open Learning Initiative (OLI)—OLI provides course materials that can be used as a textbook or supplemental material for a reduced student fee. https://oli.cmu.edu
- Open SUNY Textbooks—A catalog of open textbooks authored and peer-reviewed by SUNY (State University of New York) faculty and staff. https://textbooks.opensuny.org
- Open Textbook Library—The Open Textbook Library provides a growing catalog of free, peer-reviewed, and openly licensed textbooks. https://open.umn.edu/opentextbooks
- OpenCourseWare from MIT—MIT OpenCourseWare (OCW) is a web-based publication of virtually all MIT course content. https://ocw.mit.edu/index.htm

- Openstax CNX—OpenStax publishes high-quality, peer-reviewed, openly licensed textbooks that are absolutely free online and low cost in print. https://cnx.org
- Saylor Academy—Textbooks offered by Saylor Academy are available. Saylor also creates open online courses. https://www.saylor.org/books
- The Orange Grove—Florida's OER repository for K-12 and higher education resources. https://florida.theorangegrove.org/og/home.do
- Washington State's Open Course Library—Provides access to free or low-cost items to use in the classroom including syllabi, course activities, readings, and assessments. https://www.openwa.org/open-course-library
- WISC-Online—A collection of learning objects developed primarily by subject matter experts from the Wisconsin Technical College System (WTCS). https://www.wisc-online.com

There are also groups that have formed to promote and advance OER.

- Community College Consortium for Open Educational Resources (CCCOER)—CCCOER is a growing consortium of community and technical colleges committed to expanding access to education and increasing student success through the adoption of open educational policy, practices, and resources. CCCOER provides a community and resources to learn about the evolving practice of open education. It was founded in 2007 and has hundreds of member institutions across North America. https://www.cccoer.org
- Open Professionals Education Network (OPEN)—**OPEN** is funded by the Bill & Melinda Gates Foundation and offers free services aligned to help TAACCCT grantees meet **OER**, **accessibility**, and **quality** requirements for grant deliverables in the US Department of Labor's Trade Adjustment Assistance Community College & Career Training (TAACCCT) program. Members are those institutions under the TAACCCT grant. https://open4us.org
- Open Education Consortium—The Open Education Consortium (OEC) is a non-profit, global, member-based network of open education institutions and organizations. OEC represents its members and provides advocacy and leadership around the advancement of open education globally. It has a diverse membership from K-12 institutions to higher education institutions to nonprofits. https://www.oeconsortium.org
- Scholarly Publishing and Academic Resources Coalition (SPARC)—SPARC promotes policies and practices that enhance open access, open data, and open education. It works to enable the open sharing of research outputs and educational materials in order to democratize access to knowledge, accelerate discovery, and increase the return on investment in research and education. SPARC was formed in 1998 and has more than 200 higher education member institutions across the United States and Canada. There are also international affiliate SPARC organizations in Europe, Japan, and Africa. https://sparcopen.org

As can be seen in the growing body of literature as well as the numerous repositories and groups focused on OER, the idea of freely available course materials is one that continues to gain momentum in higher education. Libraries are not newcomers to this area, so there is an opportunity to learn from the early adopters. The survey discussed below provides insight into OER initiatives that are currently underway for both libraries that have OER initiatives and those that are considering such initiatives.

References

Achieving the Dream launches a major national initiative to help 38 community colleges in 13 states develop new degree programs using open educational resources. (2016, June 14). Retrieved from https://www.achievingthedream.org/press_release/15982/achieving-the-dream-launches-major-national-initiative-to-help-38-community-colleges-in-13-states-develop-new-degree-programs-using-open-educational-resources

Allen, N., Bell, S., & Billings, M. (2014). Spreading the word, building a community: Vision for a national librarian OER movement. *Against the Grain, 26*(5).

Anderson, T., Gaines, A., Leachman, C., & Williamson, E. P. (2017). Faculty and instructor perceptions of open educational resources in engineering. *The Reference Librarian 58*(4), 257–277.

Bell, S. (2015). Start a textbook revolution, continued: Librarians lead the way with open educational resources. *Library Issues, 35*(5), 1–4.

Bell, S. (2018). Course materials adoption: A faculty survey and outlook for the OER landscape. ACRL/Choice White Paper.

Billings, M. S., Hutton, S. C., Schafer, J., Schweik, C. M., & Sheridan, M. (2012). Open educational resources as learning materials: Prospects and strategies for university libraries. *Research Library Issues, 280*, 2–10.

Bober, C. (2017). Open educational resources: An annotated bibliography for librarians. *Education Libraries, 40*(1).

Braddlee, D., & VanScoy, A. (2019). Bridging the chasm: Faculty support roles for academic librarians in the adoption of open educational resources. *College & Research Libraries 80*(4), 426–449.

Bueno-de-la-Fuente, G., Robertson, R. J., & Boon, S. (2012). The roles of libraries and information professionals in open educational resources (OER) initiatives. JISC CETIS.

College Board. (2019). *Quick Guide: College Costs*. Retrieved from https://bigfuture.collegeboard.org/pay-for-college/college-costs/quick-guide-college-costs

Colson, R., Scott, E., & Donaldson, R. (2017). Supporting librarians in making the business case for OER. *The Reference Librarian 58*(4), 278–287.

Creative Commons. (2019). *Licensing types*. Retrieved from https://creativecommons.org/share-your-work/licensing-types-examples/

Crissinger, S. (2015). A critical take on OER practices: Interrogating commercialization, colonialism, and content. *In the Library with the Lead Pipe*, October.

Davis, E. L., Fagerheim, B., Thoms, B. L., & Cochran, D. (2016). Enhancing teaching & learning: Libraries and open educational resources in the classroom. *Public Services Quarterly, 12*(1), 22–35.

Doan, T. (2017). Why not OERs? *portal: Libraries and the Academy, 17*(4), 665–669.

Elliott, C. & Fabbro, E. (2015). The open library at AU (Athabasca University): Supporting open access and open educational resources. *Open Praxis, 7*(2), 133–140.

Enrique Perez, J. (2017). Images and the open educational resources (OER) movement. *The Reference Librarian, 58*(4), 229–237.

Ferguson, C. L. (2016). Textbooks in academic libraries. *Serials Review, 42*(3), 252–258.

Florida Virtual Campus Office of Distance Learning & Student Services. (2016). *2016 Student textbook and course materials survey.* Retrieved from http://www.openaccesstextbooks.org/pdf/2016_Florida_Student_Textbook_Survey.pdf

Goodsett, M., Loomis, B., & Miles, M. (2016). The more we work together: Leading campus OER initiatives through library-faculty collaboration. *College & Undergraduate Libraries, 23*(3), 335–342.

Griffiths, R., Gardner, S., Lundh, P., Shear, L., Ball, A., Mislevy, J., Wang, S., Desrochers, D., & Staisloff, R. (2018). *Participant experiences and financial impacts: Findings from year 2 of Achieving the Dream's OER Degree Initiative.* Menlo Park, CA: SRI International.

Hess, J. I., Nann, A. J., & Riddle, K. E. (2016). Navigating OER: The library's role in bringing OER to campus. *The Serials Librarian, 70*(1-4), 128–134.

Hilton, J. (2016). Open educational resources and college textbook choices: A review of research on efficacy and perceptions. *Educational Technology Research and Development, 64*, 573–590.

Jensen, K., & West, Q. (2015). Open educational resources and the higher education environment. *College & Research*

Libraries News, 76(4), 215–218.

Lyons, C. (2014). Library roles with textbook affordability. *Against the Grain, 26*(5), 1, 12.

Massis, B. (2016). Libraries and OER. *New Library World, 117*(11-12), 768–771.

Mitchell, C., & Chu, M. (2014). Open education resources: The new paradigm in academic libraries. *Journal of Library Innovation, 5*(1), 13–29.

Nagar, R., & Hallam-Miller, J. (2019). Open educational resources. *Tips and Trends ACRL Instruction Section.*

Okamoto, K. (2013). Making higher education more affordable, one course reading at a time: Academic libraries as key advocates for open access textbooks and educational resources. *Public Services Quarterly, 9*(4), 267–283.

Pitcher, K. (2014). Library publishing of open textbooks: The Open SUNY textbooks program. *Against the Grain, 26*(5), 22–25.

Popken, Ben. (2015, August 6). College textbook prices have risen 1,041 percent since 1977. *NBC News.* Retrieved from https://www.nbcnews.com/feature/freshman-year/college-textbook-prices-have-risen-812-percent-1978-n399926

Salam, J. A. Jr. (2017). Open pathways to student success: Academic library partnerships for open educational resource and affordable course content creation and adoption. *Journal of Academic Librarianship, 43,* 34–38.

Schmidt-Jones, C. A. (2012). An open educational resource supports a diversity of inquiry-based learning. *The International Review of Research in Open and Distance Learning, 13*(1), 1–16.

Seaman, J. E. & Seaman, J. (2018). Freeing the textbook: Educational Resources in U.S. Higher Education, 2018. Babson Survey Research Group. Retrieved from https://www.onlinelearningsurvey.com/reports/freeingthetextbook2018.pdf

Seneck, E. (2014). Fixing the broken textbook market: How students respond to high textbook costs and demand alternatives. U.S. PIRG Education Fund & The Student PIRGs. Retrieved from https://uspirg.org/sites/pirg/files/reports/NATIONAL%20Fixing%20Broken%20Textbooks%20Report1.pdf

Shank, J. D. (2014). *Interactive open educational resources.* Jossey-Bass: San Francisco, CA.

Smith, B., & Lee, L. (2017). Librarians and OER: Cultivating a community of practice to be more effective advocates. *Journal of Library & Information Services in Distance Learning, 11*(1-2), 106–122.

Smith, M. S., & Casserly, C. M. (2006). The promise of open educational resources. *Change, 38*(5), 8–17.

Sutton, S. C., & Chadwell, F. A. (2014). Open textbooks at Oregon State University: A case study of new opportunities for academic libraries and university presses. *Journal of Librarianship and Scholarly Communication, 2*(4). http://doi.org/10.7710/2162-3309.1174.

Todorinova, L., & Wilkinson, Z. T. (2019). Closing the loop: Students, academic libraries, and textbook affordability. *Journal of Academic Librarianship, 45*(3), 268–277.

UNESCO. (2002). UNESCO promotes new initiative for free educational resources on the internet. *United Nations Educational, Scientific and Cultural Organization.* Paris, France.

UNESCO. (2019). Open educational resources. Retrieved from https://en.unesco.org/themes/building-knowledge-societies/oer

United States Government Accounting Office. (2013). *College textbooks: Students have greater access to textbook information (GAO-13-368).* Washington DC: US Government Accounting Office. Retrieved from https://www.gao.gov/products/GAO-13-368

Walz, A. R. (2015). Exploring library engagement in open educational resource adoption, adaption and authoring. *Virginia Libraries, 61,* 23–31.

Walz, A., Jensen, K., & Salem, J. A. Jr. (2016). SPEC Kit 351: Affordable course content and open educational resources. *Association of Research Libraries.*

Wiley, D. (n.d.). Defining the "open" in open content. *Open content.* Retrieved from http://opencontent.org/definition.

ANALYSIS AND DISCUSSION OF SURVEY RESULTS

The survey gathered information on the current status of OER initiatives at colleges and small universities. After first establishing the frequency of such initiatives, it was meant to probe into the details of such initiatives. This allowed for a comparison of the initiatives and provides other institutions considering OER an overview of the types of activities that take place with such programs. Respondents were allowed several opportunities to provide comments in the survey as the qualitative thoughts related to the benefits, challenges, and opportunities of OER would be helpful for others moving forward.

The survey was sent via email using a list of ACRL contacts at college and small university libraries. There were 1,103 libraries on the list. The emails to fifty-five institutions were not delivered, leaving a survey pool of 1,047 possible respondents. The survey was opened on April 24, 2019, and closed on June 10, 2019. A reminder email was sent in the middle of the survey period. Of the possible 1,047 respondents, 204 individuals submitted answers to the survey questions. This was a 19.48 percent response rate. The questions were all optional, resulting in a range in the number of responses to each individual question.

Respondents were from the following Carnegie classifications: Master's small programs (32.34 percent), Baccalaureate Arts & Sciences (25.75 percent), Master's medium programs (13.77 percent), Baccalaureate: Diverse Fields (11.8 percent), Master's large programs (7.19 percent), other (5.39 percent), and Baccalaureate/Associates (3.59 percent). The majority of respondents were from private institutions at 69 percent and 31 percent at public institutions.

The range of FTE students was 200 to 35,420. Average FTE students across respondents was 3,228 with a median of 2,100 and a mode of 1,200 and 1,400. Staffing levels also varied. Respondents reported an average of 5.9 librarians with a range from 1 to 34. The median was 5 and the mode was 2. Respondents also reported an average of 5.7 support staff with a range from 0 to 29. The median was 4 and the mode was 1.

When asked if their library has taken part in an OER initiative, 44 percent responded yes, 19 percent said an initiative is currently under development, 16 percent said no but that there were plans for an initiative, and 21 percent said no and that there were no plans for an initiative. The positive response to this question is expected as you are more likely to complete a survey when you have some experience on the topic. However, even when looking at the raw numbers, we know that at least 10 percent of the possible 1,047 respondents either have an OER initiative on their campus or an initiative is under development.

This shows that OER is not an isolated phenomenon but rather something that is being done across a range of institutions. Of the seventy-three libraries reporting that they have taken part in an OER initiative on their campus, nineteen are from Baccalaureate Arts & Sciences, one from Baccalaureate/Associates, ten from Baccalaureate: Diverse Fields, four from Master's large programs, eleven from Master's medium programs, twenty-three from Master's small program, and five from other programs. These numbers match up with the overall numbers of respondents. The split of respondents who noted they have taken part in the OER initiative on their campus is again representative with the overall numbers in that 53 percent are from a private institution and 47 percent are from a public institution.

Funding is a major issue in any initiative, and when asked where funding came from, the most frequent sources included the library's general budget (20 percent), an external grant (18 percent), the institution's general budget (13 percent), and the institution's special project budget (10 percent). The largest number of respondents noted funding came from a source other than those that were listed (31 percent). The most commonly occurring source was through a library consortium, usually at the state level. For these initiatives to continue, it may be important to ensure that they have consistent funding in the future. Outside grants can be used to start a program, but they rarely provide long-term continuing support. It may also be unrealistic to expect libraries to fund these initiatives without other financial support.

These funds were used for a number of items. The most common was faculty incentives, which was noted by 44 percent of those responding. Other listed expenditures were more evenly noted and include software (19 percent), faculty course release time (7 percent), library staff (7 percent), equipment (6 percent), and technical support staff (4 percent). Within the "other" category, some items included training, professional development, travel, editorial services, course reserves purchases, and membership in OER groups. The funds are most frequently used for faculty incentives and stipends. It needs to be considered whether funding will continue to be available long-term to pay faculty and whether other items such as maintenance of OER will require more support in the future when there are more resources that must be managed.

Faculty are encouraged to take part in OER initiatives most frequently through the offering of financial stipends. This was noted by 45 percent of the respondents. Another frequently occurring incentive was offering instructional design assistance, which was noted by 30 percent of the respondents. Also offered were course release time and promotion/tenure credit, both with 5 percent. Respondents were also asked if the faculty received financial incentives what was the average amount received. These amounts varied between initiatives and within the level of participation within a single institution. For example, one respondent noted faculty received $500 to investigate OER, $1,000 or more if implemented, and $5,800 or a course release to create an OER. Overall responses varied from a low of $100 to a high of $5,800. Although the ranges given provide some fuzziness in the reporting, in general, the average amount noted by respondents was $1,071 with a median of $750 and a mode of $500.

Respondents were then asked about what types of resources faculty had adopted, adapted, or created for the OER initiative. Textbooks were the most common with 37 percent of the respondents noting their use. Course readings/articles were not far behind with 31 percent. Following those were videos at 13 percent and multimedia at 11 percent. Given the traditional structure of assigning a textbook for a course, these results were not surprising. It may be interesting to see if the ability to pick and choose OER content results in more mixed resources in the future.

Assessment of the OER initiatives is critical in determining effectiveness. Twenty-six percent of respondents noted that there has been no assessment of OER initiatives, 25 percent of respondents noted there had been assessment, with the remaining 48 percent noting there had been no assessment to date but plans were underway. For those that had assessed their OER initiatives, several metrics were utilized. These included the number of dollars saved by students (27 percent), number of faculty using OER (21 percent), number of students using OER (20 percent), grades/academic achievement of students (9 percent), increase in student retention (8 percent), increase in course completion (5 percent), and reduction in course drops (5 percent). It is encouraging that around 75 percent of respondents have either started assessment or are planning their assessment strategies. The types of assessments that are taking place are not surprising. Cost savings and numbers of individuals involved are readily available metrics. The metrics related to academic achievement will require a more focused research approach.

The survey then shifted from the OER initiative as a whole to the library's activities related to the initiative. Given a listing of supporting services, respondents noted whether they provided the service, planned to provide the service in the future, or did not provide nor planned to provide the service. The most commonly offered service was support for identifying OER and/or affordable content. This was provided by 84 percent with 15 percent planning to provide. Other common services included copyright and/or open licensing consultation (71 percent / 16 percent), electronic access for OER in an institutional repository or other online system (44 percent / 39 percent), and education services on OER topics (workshops, faculty development sessions, etc.) (63 percent / 28 percent). Services that were not as common include collaborating with student groups, funding, software systems to support publication of OER books and other materials, staff support for the publication of books and other learning objects (editing, formatting, and other publication services), and instructional design support.

For those that provided or planned to provide educational services, they were asked what topics are covered. There was a range of topics, including how/where to find open materials (22 percent), open licensing (20 percent), how/where to deposit open materials (14 percent), author's rights (12 percent), open publishing (12 percent), innovative pedagogy (12 percent), and copyright negotiation (8 percent).

When asked how much time the library spends on the initiative, the most frequent response was a couple of hours every week with 42 percent of respondents, the next was a couple of hours every month with 41 percent of the respondents, and the last was a couple of hours every day with 17 percent of the respondents. This highlights that while there are a number of OER initiatives in place, there are not many librarians dedicated to the initiatives. This is reinforced in the comments provided later that note how with small staff numbers it is hard to provide much time for OER.

Respondents were then asked what skills, knowledge, and abilities are necessary for librarians working with OER initiatives: being able to search successfully for OER resources (23 percent), intellectual property/copyright/open licensing issues (22 percent), assessment (14 percent), project management (14 percent), scholarly publishing and communication processes (14 percent), publishing skills (5 percent), and editorial skills (5 percent). Within the "other" category, some of them included marketing, promotion, and the ability to work with others across campus. The most common skills and abilities listed by respondents fall under skills that are often held by librarians. The focus on skills already possessed by librarians is highlighted when respondents discuss how librarians have the ability to lead OER initiatives.

Respondents then shared a brief example of a successful library collaboration with an OER initiative. There were a number of excellent examples that highlighted how OER can take different forms across a range of situations. Some of the themes that emerged included libraries providing access to OER materials. This varied from simply providing websites that link to OER resources to "a librarian provided the department with a spreadsheet that identified a variety of open access textbooks on various platforms (OTN, OpenStax, etc.), the authors, and feedback on the potential ease of using each title or platform."

Libraries also provided a variety of professional development opportunities for faculty. There were a number of respondents who noted they held workshops for faculty and a two-day OER bootcamp; a couple of them went deeper by establishing faculty learning communities on OER. Librarians also helped several faculty with technical aspects in either the creation or implementation of an OER. There was a mix of respondents either describing a one-to-one or one-to-many process of working with faculty.

In describing successes, several respondents noted the savings for students with the use of OER. "The rolling impact from the 2018 institute totals approximately $132,000 in annual student savings." "The course switched from a ~$150 textbook from which only a few chapters were used to a single free resource that is 100% relevant to the course." "One of our engineering faculty members developed an online course text to replace his required textbook, which normally cost about $198. Approximately 25 students enroll in his course each semester; with this resource, he saves each class nearly $5,000 in textbook costs." "Using conservative calculations, this $25,000 grant has resulted in a savings of 2.5 million dollars in student textbook costs."

Next, respondents shared their thoughts on the role of libraries with OER. While there was some variety in the responses, overall, the comments noted the connection between OER and libraries. Several respondents noted that libraries should take a leadership role in OER. They noted how libraries are at the forefront of OER due to their knowledge and experience in a number of areas such as author rights, dissemination of scholarly research, copyright information, instruction, access to needed materials, finding information, creating web directories for resources, and publishing. There were some responses which while noting the services of the library, stressed the fact that the library cannot undertake OER on its own. Partnerships need to be made with others across campus, not only with faculty members but also with other departments such as learning centers, provosts, and curriculum centers. There were comments which noted that these partnerships were especially important because with limited staff and funding it was not possible for the library to take on OER alone.

Respondents then provided final thoughts on OER. While the answers to the previous question were very positive, the answers to this question were tempered. Several comments discussed how it can be difficult to establish OER. There may be funding issues, buy-in issues from faculty and administration, or simply a lack of time. However, the comments overall noted the importance of OER. Several discussed the social justice issue of OER, noting the high cost paid by students and how it is important to do everything possible to lower the expense. There were also a number of comments discussing the publishing industry. It was stated that libraries need to work against publishing monopolies that have raised textbook costs. Also of concern was the idea that OER would find themselves under the control of such groups.

There were also comments that talked about the need to ensure consistency and updating of OER. "I am concerned about the ephemeral nature of OER websites. In the last year alone, many of the 'go to' websites for OER content have shut down or moved locations. It's becoming increasingly challenging to keep links for these resources up-to-date when they keep disappearing. It also adds to the perception among some faculty that OER are not "serious publications." "The invisible labor of OER needs to be addressed to ensure that OER is a sustainable model" was another concern respondents raised. "I feel a bit uneasy about the lack of compensation for authors in the OER sphere. I am concerned that OER production will become another facet of volunteer service for certain faculty (most likely women, junior and contingent faculty, and students), but better connected faculty (usually men and other senior faculty) will continue to get lucrative contracts with commercial publishers." Finally, an important grouping of comments noted how OER is not a solution to all problems and that the resources need to be a part of a larger systematic approach to education. Pedagogy needs to be considered when utilizing OER.

The survey showed that OER initiatives are increasingly becoming a part of the daily work of librarians at colleges and small universities. The responsibilities related to these initiatives vary, but there is an overall belief in the importance of OER as a concept, and the related support offered by the library is seen as a positive addition for the field. The addition of new programmatic initiatives requires each institution to consider how institutional support and priorities fit into the established workload of the library. OER will remain an issue within higher education and libraries must reflect on their connection to it.

APPENDIX A. SURVEY WITH RESULTS

Q. Carnegie classifications of participating institutions.

(Carnegie Classification Descriptions of the categories can be found at http://carnegieclassifications.iu.edu/classification_descriptions/basic.php)

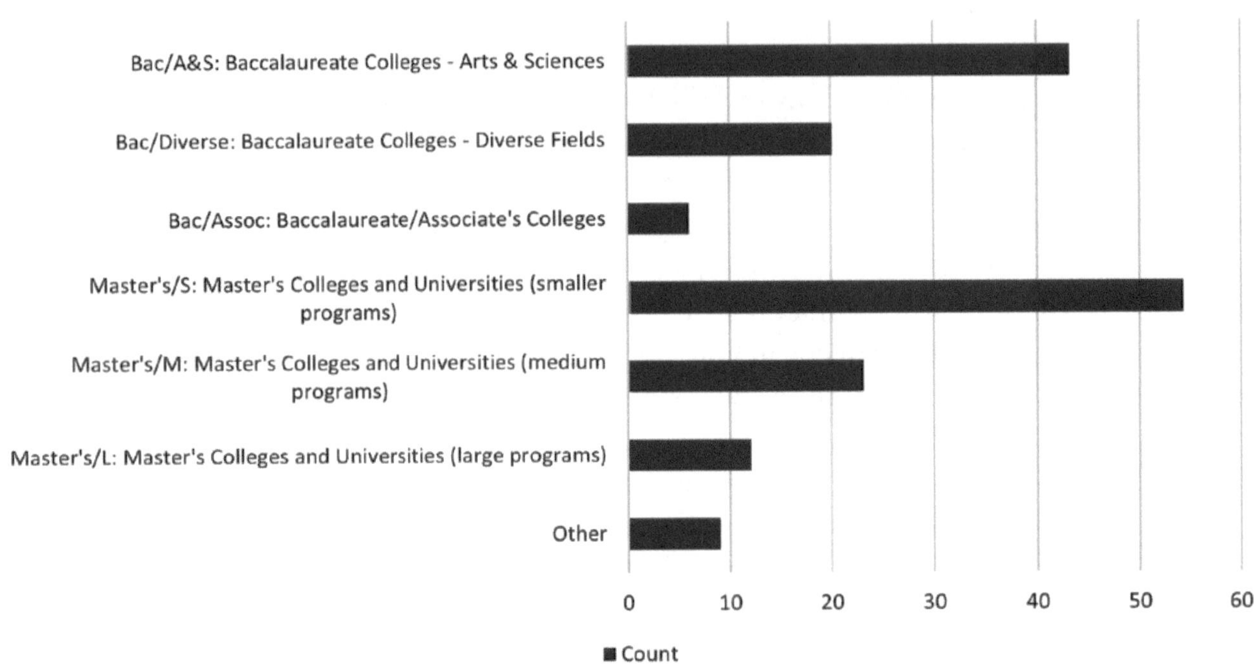

Responses	%	Count
Bac/A&S: Baccalaureate Colleges—Arts & Sciences	25.75%	43
Bac/Diverse: Baccalaureate Colleges—Diverse Fields	11.98%	20
Bac/Assoc: Baccalaureate/Associate's Colleges	3.59%	6
Master's/S: Master's Colleges and Universities (smaller programs)	32.34%	54
Master's/M: Master's Colleges and Universities (medium programs)	13.77%	23
Master's/L: Master's Colleges and Universities (large programs)	7.19%	12
Other	5.39%	9
Total:	100%	167

Q. Type of Institution

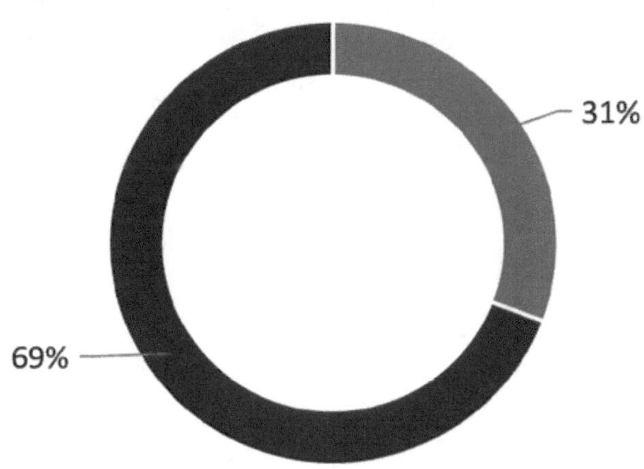

Responses	%	Count
Public	30.72%	51
Private	69.28%	115
Total:	100%	166

Q. Institution Size

Responses		
FTE Students	Number of Librarians	Number of Library Support Staff
986	2	3
6,771	14	10
15,100	10	10
1,500	5	1.5
3,002	5	9
n/a	10	11
3,300	3	4
3,397	6	2
1,200	3	1
5,407	13	12
1,100	2	1
3,100	3	2
8,455	7	8

Responses		
FTE Students	Number of Librarians	Number of Library Support Staff
1,200	2.7	4.7
1,441	3	2
4,800	9	24
3,400	6	7
4,026	10	10
1,400	2	8
3,160	5	3
5,200	6	12
1,275	1	8
993	6	3.5
2,896	5	2
3,320	7	10
7,315	15	20

Responses		
FTE Students	**Number of Librarians**	**Number of Library Support Staff**
10,872	24	20
8,400	20	13
2,004	6	6
3,700	10	12
2,100	10	15
672	1	1
573	2	4
1,800	12	10
5,000	9	9
	1.8	2
2,480	13	11
4,200	6	5
1,700	5	5
750	3	2
2,000	2	2
2,600	13	13
3,500	8	25
2,500	5	2
1,780	9	10
1,350	3.5	2.5
1,400	1	2
1,200	2	1
550	1	1
4,103	4.2	2.2
2,600	6	2
1,280	3	7
2,571	5	3
2,018	3.5	2
1,475	6	6
2,700	5	5
2,504	11	8

Responses		
FTE Students	**Number of Librarians**	**Number of Library Support Staff**
1,750	7	12
	4	2.5
1,400	3.5	3
3,600	5	7
516	2	3
4,609	5.5	8.5
3,000	5	4
9,972	14	15
1,482	4	7
1,679	9.5	4.43
5,000	10	
655	1	1
5,000	3	1
2,076	6	5
1,082	3	2
2,250	8	3
8,000	7	15
1,813	13	13
4,600	8	10
2,640	5	4
35,420	34	29
1,500	3	6
4,800	8	12
1,200	3	2
740	1	1
2,400	7	5
8,800	4	0
3,300	4	0
3,900	3	7
4,300	7	8
1,565	4	3

Responses		
FTE Students	Number of Librarians	Number of Library Support Staff
1,800	6	3
2,750	2	1
1,180	3.25	0
6,263	8	7
5,408	8	5
517	2	1
2,200	5	8
200	1	1
1,411	2.50	2.74
1,300	1	31/2
4,100	7	5
10,000	9	11
1,800	5	3
11,071	19	9
2,600	10	15
700	2	1
2,039	13	10
1,500	6.5	2
5,700	11	5
2,800	11	10
24,000	4	2
5	2	3
2,100	13	23
4,400	8	4
~5,800	9	12
3,000	4	4
705	2	3
2,100	6.5 FTE	3 FTE
1,106	3	20 student workers, no staff
8,617	10	6.5

Responses		
FTE Students	Number of Librarians	Number of Library Support Staff
2,400	7	7
1,065	2	2
487	2	1
2,200	6	5
1,932	5	5
1,310	3	4
3,719	6	7
2,800	8.5	4.5
2,500	5	1
2,010	4.5	3
650	2	1
1,151	2	2.5
1,528	3	7
1,556	4	3
1,950	1	0
9,046	15	15
800	2	2
6,089	7	10
1,780	4	3
3,972	6	2
231	1	0
954	3	2
1,080	1.3	2.6
8,313	12	13
2,410	10	8
3,000	3	3
1,900	2	1
2,300	8	4
1,300	2	1
2,291	7	5.7

Responses		
FTE Students	Number of Librarians	Number of Library Support Staff
2,308	3	0, excluding student workers
4,000	10	25
1,000	3	1
580	4	3.75
1,555	4	1
1,661	4	1
1,987	6	7
1,100	3	1.5
818	1	1.7

Responses		
FTE Students	Number of Librarians	Number of Library Support Staff
1,383	3	2.6
1,400	5.5	1.5
2,775	7	7
546	2	1
3,900	2	9
2,593	8 FTE	1.5
1,060	3	1
958	2	1.5
2,419	8	4
1,171	5	4

Q. Has your library taken part in an initiative that is focused on encouraging faculty to adopt, adapt, or create affordable course content/open educational resources for teaching and learning?

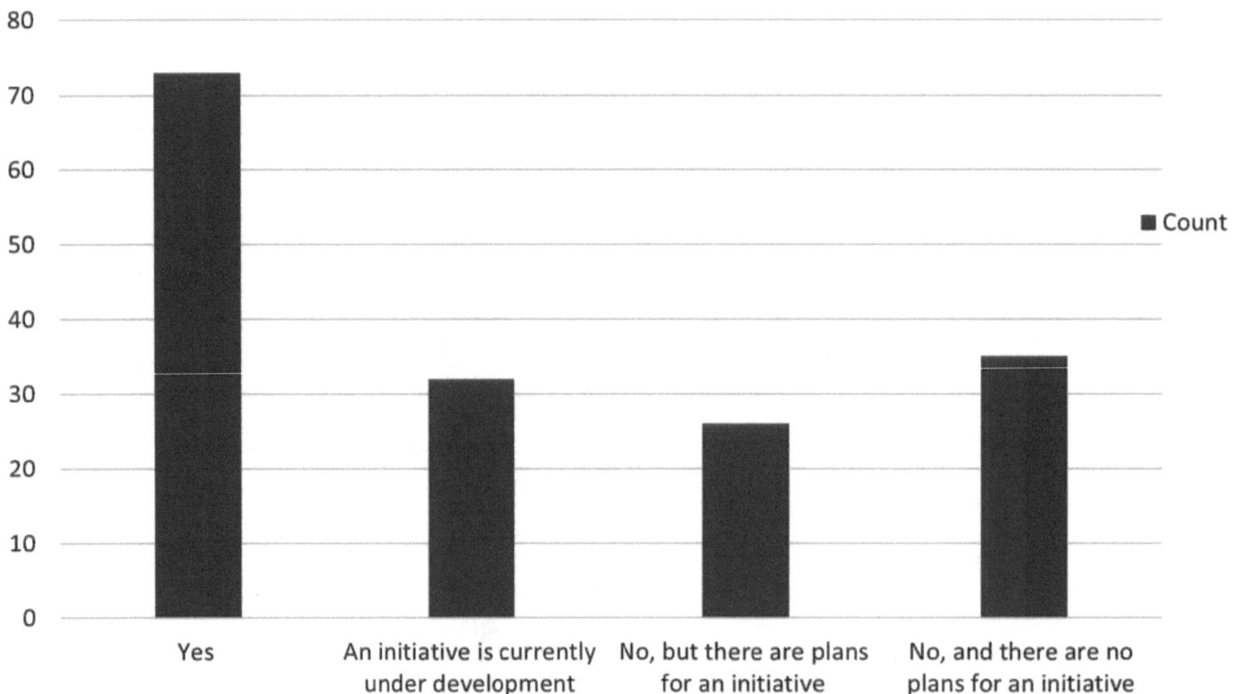

Responses	%	Count
Yes	43.98%	73
An initiative is currently under development	19.28%	32
No, but there are plans for an initiative	15.66%	26
No, and there are no plans for an initiative	21.08%	35
Total:	100%	166

Q. Where did funding come from?

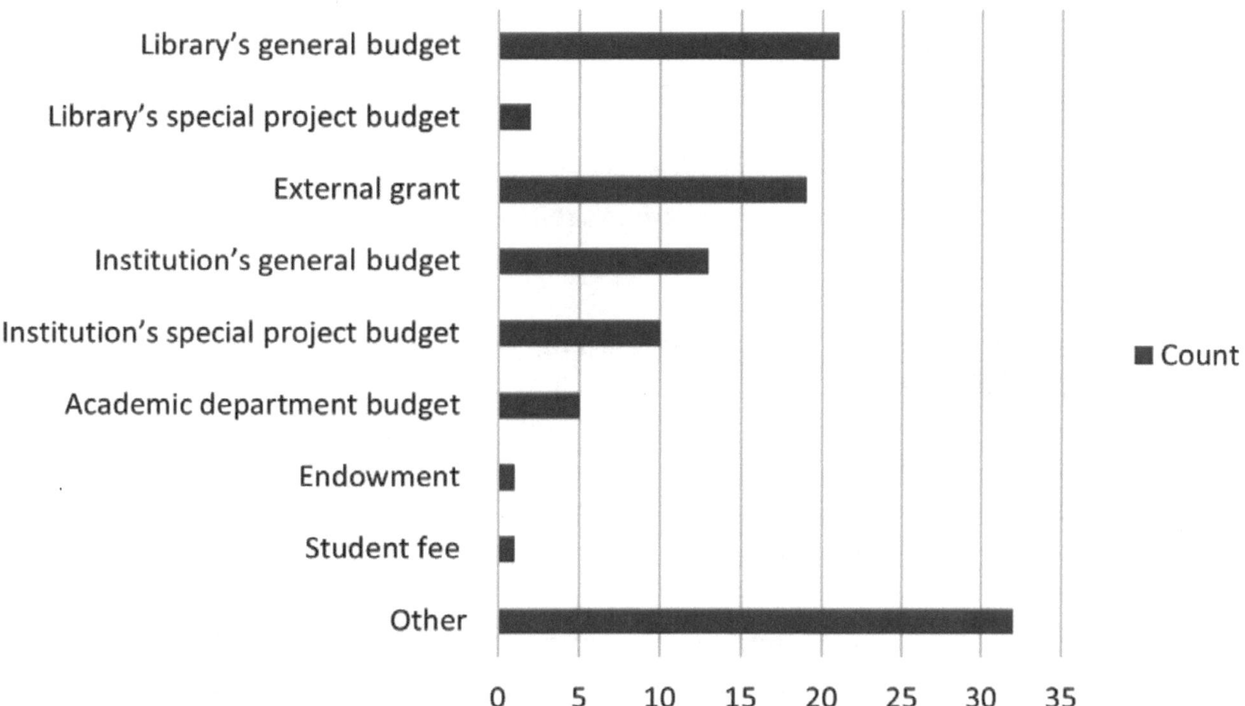

Responses	%	Count
Library's general budget	20.19%	21
Library's special project budget	1.92%	2
External grant	18.27%	19
Institution's general budget	12.50%	13
Institution's special project budget	9.62%	10
Academic department budget	4.81%	5
Endowment	0.96%	1
Student fee	0.96%	1
Other (see below)	30.77%	32
Total:	100%	104

"Other" responses:

- Consortial initiative
- No
- Donor
- The VIVA consortium (academic libraries in VA) has faculty grants to support adoption or creation of OER
- Also subsidized by the Student Tech Fee
- Provost's office
- State funding (to SUNY system)
- Shared among D of Fac, D of College, Aca Resource Center (tutoring, etc.) and Library
- Grant from student government association
- We conducted a joint OER Faculty Review Program with Duke University, Davidson College, and Johnson C. Smith University which are all Duke Endowment institutions. The money came from a fund set aside for group projects conducted by the Duke Endowed libraries
- No funding designated for this initiative
- Budget for our Center for Teaching and Learning
- Office of Online Learning
- An initiative from the University System of Georgia called Affordable Learning Georgia
- Source hasn't been identified yet
- Library consortium (VIVA—Virginia)
- An allocation from the NY State budget, administered by SUNY OER Services.
- No
- University System of New Hampshire (funding goes to all 4 state colleges & universities)
- Center for Excellence of Teaching and Learning Curriculum Innovation Grants
- Still working on that
- We have a campus OER Task Force that is currently working on this.
- No funding
- Individual academic department's budget
- VIVA state-wide consortium
- NY State Legislature $4M appropriation
- No funding
- We're currently on a rental by credit hour program; the library was not involved despite asking to be involved.
- Library consortium
- Membership in statewide academic library consortium
- No current funding
- No funding

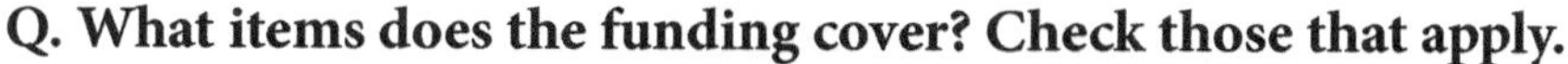

Q. What items does the funding cover? Check those that apply.

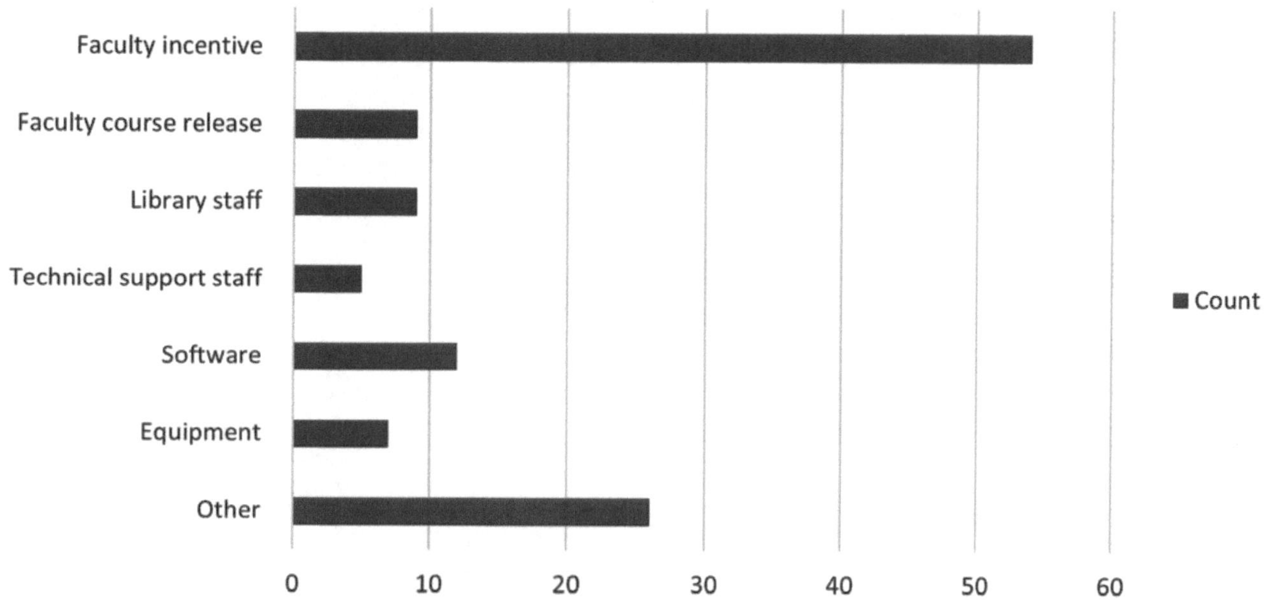

Responses	%	Count
Faculty incentive	44.26%	54
Faculty course release	7.38%	9
Library staff	7.38%	9
Technical support staff	4.10%	5
Software	9.84%	12
Equipment	5.74%	7
Other (see below)	21.31%	26
Total:	100%	122

“Other” responses:

- Encouragement to review open access textbooks
- N/A
- Cost of course reserves books
- Training, membership
- Small buyout of part of one librarian’s time (allowed for hire of part-time librarian to cover her reference desk hours)
- Copyediting or other professional assistance
- Faculty incentives are being determined now
- Staff are not additionally compensated for their work on OER
- Professional development/travel
- None
- Editorial services; training course and cohort community
- Some initial purchases & marketing

- One-time funding for membership in the Open Textbook Network; subsequent membership years will be funded through our textbook rental fee
- Course content—e-books for the classroom
- No
- Speakers for professional development events, other event expenses
- Platform expenses, layout/design, hiring student assistant
- Professional development
- Membership to a state OER consortia
- None
- Printing
- Conference travel
- We've outsourced this through Sodexo, who buys/rents on our behalf and provides the books to students directly.
- OER Coordinator for the consortium
- Training

Q. Are there any incentives that encourage faculty to adopt, adapt, or create affordable course content/open educational resources? If yes, indicate the type of incentive. Check those that apply.

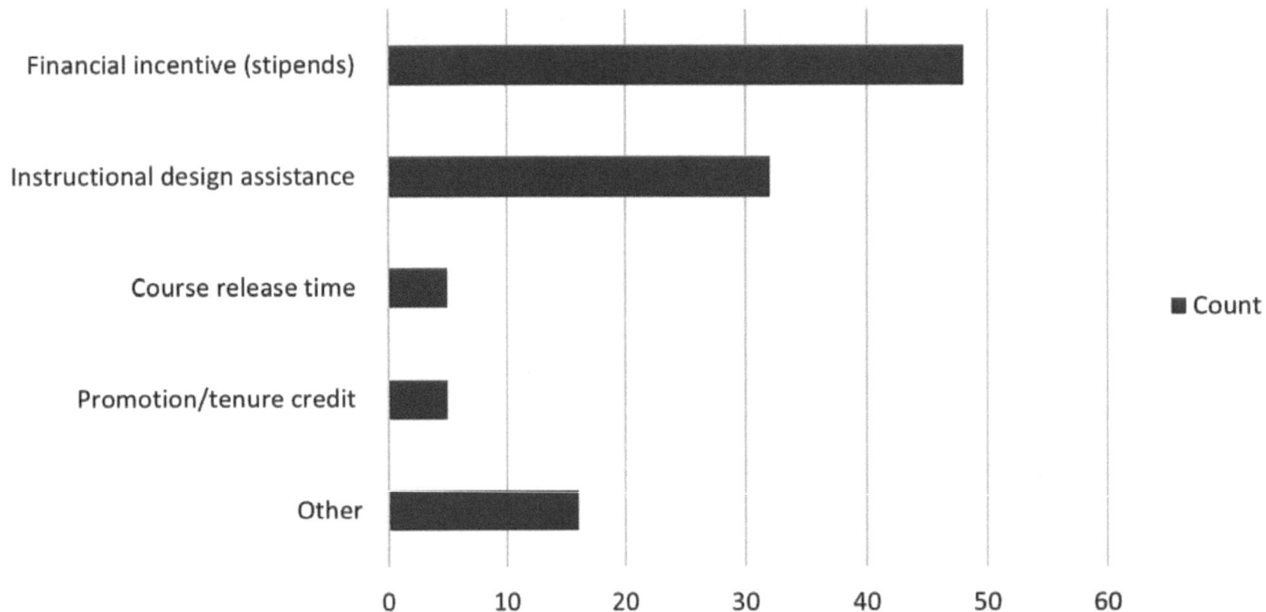

Responses	%	Count
Financial incentive (stipends)	45.28%	48
Instructional design assistance	30.19%	32
Course release time	4.72%	5
Promotion/tenure credit	4.72%	5
Other (see below)	15.09%	16
Total:	100%	106

"Other" responses:

- Statewide consortial funding
- Faculty incentives are being determined now
- Library-led summer institute
- Recognition
- None
- TRAILS Montana's Academic Library Consortia has hired an OER Coordinator who will provide support for member institutions
- Under development
- No
- Library/ ITS support
- None
- No
- Proposed but not yet created. Faculty were encouraged to use OER or library holdings this year but no incentives have yet been offered
- There are no OED initiatives at this time, but we're at the initial stages of discussing it for our MBA programs
- Faculty Development Grant
- Through the state consortium, there is an opportunity for faculty to receive up to $30K in grant money.
- Administrative challenge for no commercial textbooks in freshman courses

Q. If faculty receive financial incentives, what is the average amount received?

- $200.00
- N/A
- $1,500
- n/a
- $1,000
- $500
- $200
- $800
- $500
- $1,500
- $2,500
- $250
- $500
- Faculty incentives are being determined now
- $500 to investigate OER, $1000 more if implemented; $5,800 or course release for creation of OER
- $1,000
- $250

- $3,000 for a six-week institute
- $500
- $750 individual, $2,000 team
- $1,000
- $200
- None
- $500
- $500–$5,000
- $400
- DNK
- $5,000
- $1,000
- $100
- $1,500
- $500
- N/A
- $230
- $200 review of Open Textbooks, course redesign grants vary
- $800
- $500
- $1,500
- Depends; $1,500 for a curriculum innovation grant that includes an OER track
- $1,200
- $750
- $300
- $500–$5,000
- IDK
- $750
- $1,000
- ?
- $1,000
- N/A
- $200
- $5,000
- $500/course
- Not yet determined
- $200
- N/A
- $1,000
- $200
- I am not sure

Q. What types of resources have faculty adopted, adapted, or created as part of the initiative? Check those that apply.

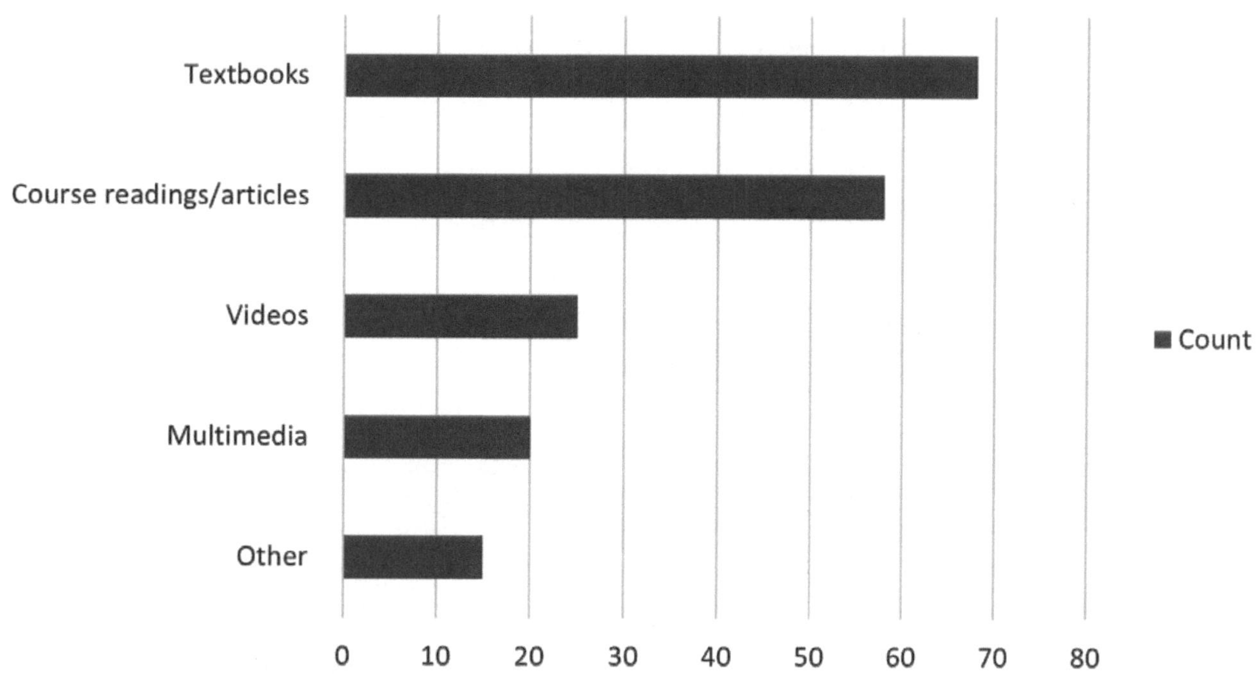

Responses	%	Count
Textbooks	36.56%	68
Course readings/articles	31.18%	58
Videos	13.44%	25
Multimedia	10.75%	20
Other (see below)	8.06%	15
Total:	100%	186

"Other" responses:

- Test bank for French classes
- Supplementary materials
- Monologue database, lab manuals, etc.
- Program just began, just completed their initial one-week intensive training program (no adoptions yet)
- We anticipate potential use of all formats
- Open source journal
- Unknown
- New initiative—some of this is "to be determined"
- Still in development
- We haven't started the initiative yet, but some faculty are using textbooks, course readings/articles, and videos already.

- Library e-books
- Ancillary materials
- Library e-books, articles, and streaming videos
- None formally to date, but they're thinking MBA course readings/materials and maybe OER textbooks
- Lab manuals

Q. Has there been any assessment on the initiative?

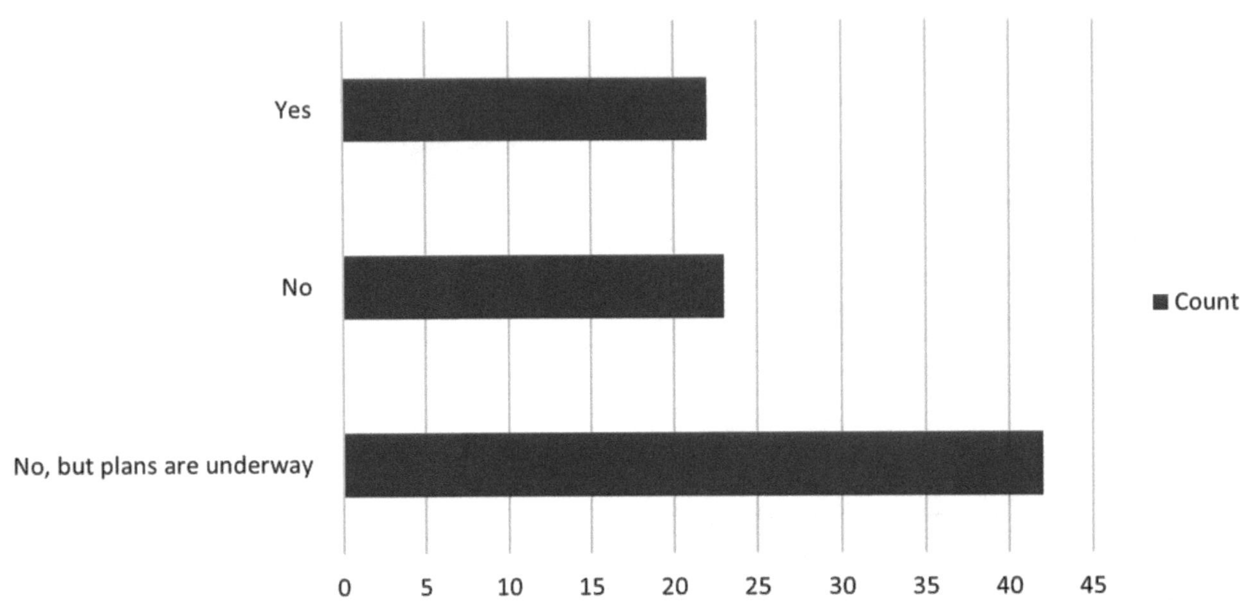

Responses	%	Count
Yes	25.29%	22
No	26.44%	23
No, but plans are underway	48.28%	42
Total:	100%	87

Q. If there has been assessment on the initiative, what metrics have been used? Check those that apply.

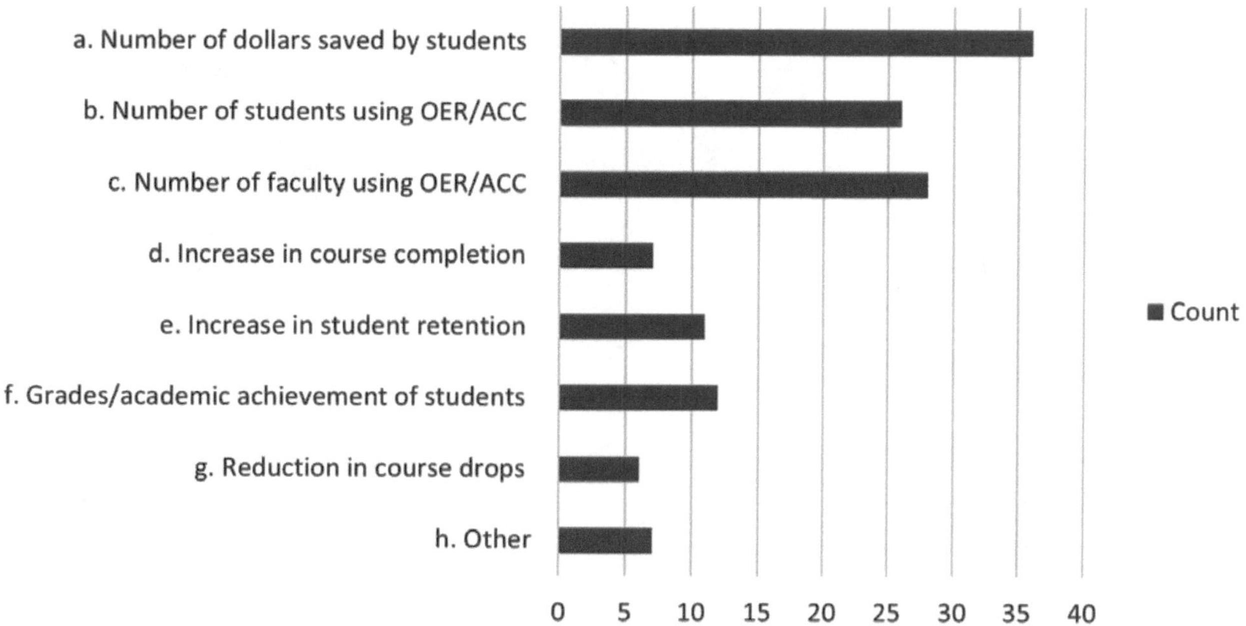

Responses	%	Count
a. Number of dollars saved by students	27.07%	36
b. Number of students using OER/ACC	19.55%	26
c. Number of faculty using OER/ACC	21.05%	28
d. Increase in course completion	5.26%	7
e. Increase in student retention	8.27%	11
f. Grades/academic achievement of students	9.02%	12
g. Reduction in course drops	4.51%	6
h. Other (see below)	5.26%	7
Total:	100%	133

"Other" responses:

- We will use at least the metrics in a, e, f, and g.
- N/A
- VIVA calculates the dollars saved for the whole state.
- We're now working with our first cohort of 11 faculty interested in creating or adopting OER. We've not decided on how to assess the program yet. The first courses using OER won't be taught until spring 2020.
- N/A
- N/A
- Are just beginning; all of the above will probably be used in some fashion.

Q. Please indicate the types of support activities/services your library currently provides or plans to provide. Check all those that apply.

Question	Responses						Total
	Provides		Plans to Provide		Neither Provides nor Plans to Provide		
a. Copyright and/or open licensing consultation	70.79%	63	15.73%	14	13.48%	12	89
b. Support for identifying OER and/or affordable content	84.27%	75	14.61%	13	1.12%	1	89
c. Electronic access for OER in an institutional repository or other online system	43.68%	38	39.08%	34	17.24%	15	87
d. Education services on OER topics (workshops, faculty development sessions, etc.)	62.92%	56	28.09%	25	8.99%	8	89
e. Collaborating with student groups	25.00%	21	36.90%	31	38.10%	32	84
f. Funding	29.76%	25	19.05%	16	51.19%	43	84
g. Software systems to support publication of OER books and other materials	19.28%	16	24.10%	20	56.63%	47	83
h. Staff support for the publication of books and other learning objects (editing, formatting, and other publication services)	17.86%	15	19.05%	16	63.10%	53	84
i. Instructional design support	35.71%	30	21.43%	18	42.86%	36	84
j. Other	16.67%	7	7.14%	3	76.19%	32	42

Q. If your library provides or plans to provide educational services to faculty, what topics are covered. Check all those that apply.

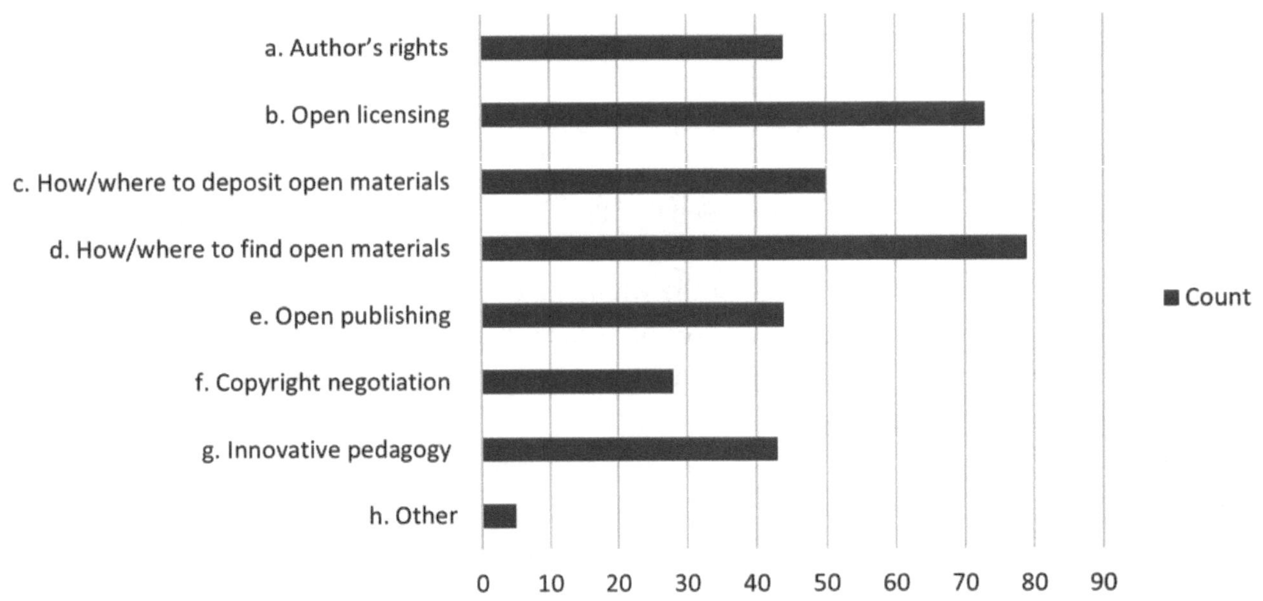

Responses	%	Count
a. Author's rights	12.02%	44
b. Open licensing	19.95%	73
c. How/where to deposit open materials	13.66%	50
d. How/where to find open materials	21.58%	79
e. Open publishing	12.02%	44
f. Copyright negotiation	7.65%	28
g. Innovative pedagogy	11.75%	43
h. Other (see below)	1.37%	5
Total:	100%	366

"Other" responses:

- Usability testing of course shells accessibility, usability
- On-campus examples, definition of, benefits of, software tools
- The university has laid off the librarian who best knows copyright. The remaining librarian may not have time or expertise to do much on copyright although she will help find open source materials.
- We've helped an institutional press with copyright negotiation and CIP issues; we've not been asked to participate in any other textbook or course material initiatives.

Q. How much time is spent by the library on this initiative?

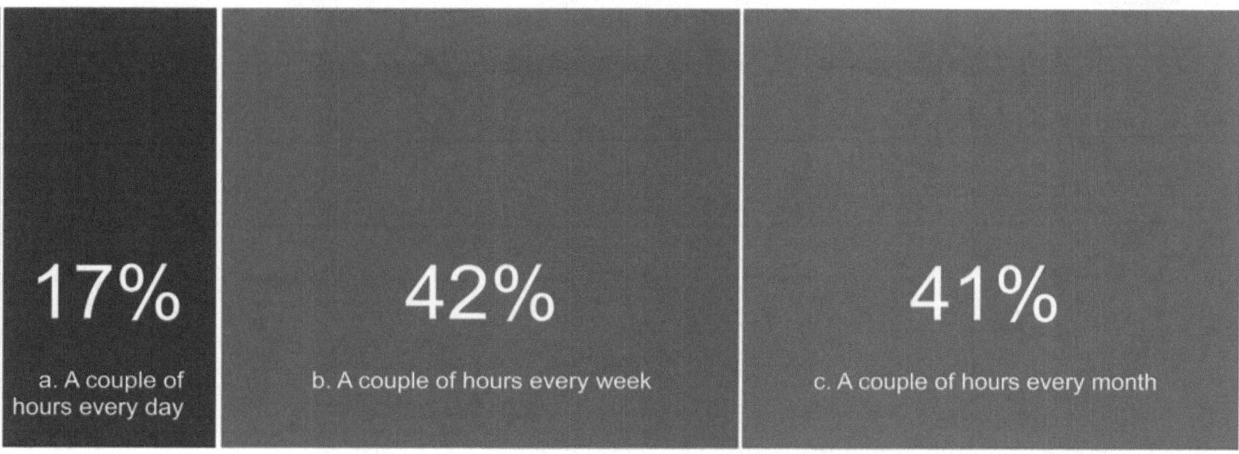

Responses	%	Count
a. A couple of hours every day	17.44%	15
b. A couple of hours every week	41.86%	36
c. A couple of hours every month	40.70%	35
Total:	100%	86

Q. Please indicate the knowledge, skills, and abilities that are necessary for the initiative. Check all those that apply.

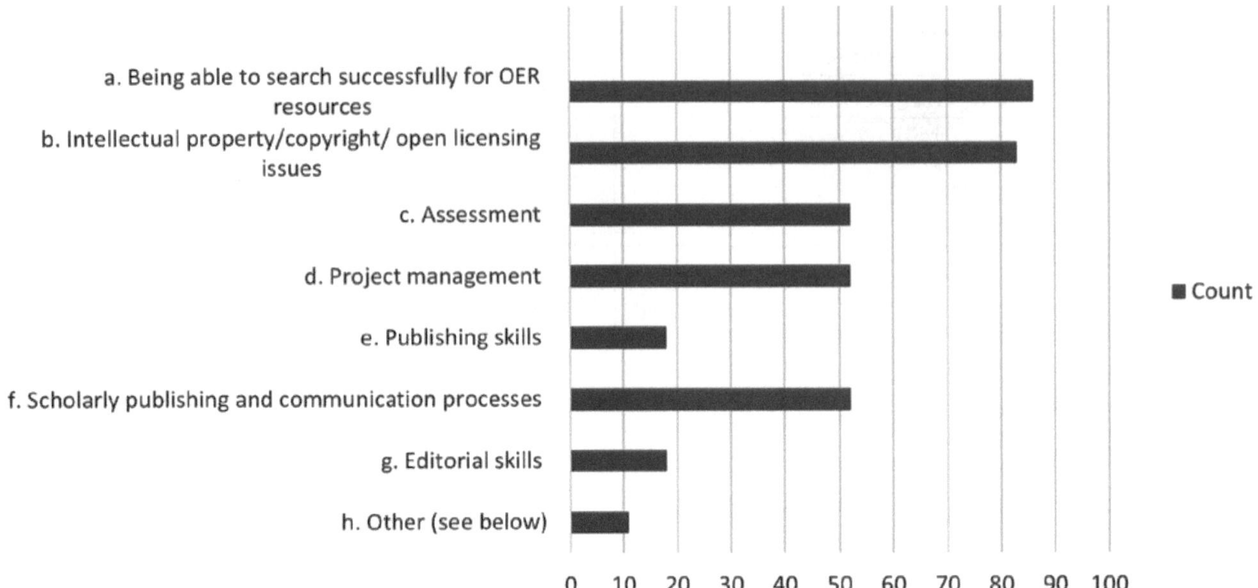

Responses	%	Count
a. Being able to search successfully for OER resources	23.12%	86
b. Intellectual property/copyright/ open licensing issues	22.31%	83
c. Assessment	13.98%	52
d. Project management	13.98%	52
e. Publishing skills	4.84%	18
f. Scholarly publishing and communication processes	13.98%	52
g. Editorial skills	4.84%	18
h. Other (see below)	2.96%	11
Total:	100%	372

"Other" responses:

- Instructional design best practices for course content delivery inter-personal skills
- Being able to convince faculty of the value of OER
- Leadership skills for working with faculty and campus administrators; knowledge of academic culture and faculty preferences and prerogatives for course material selection
- Campus networking/ promotion of OER
- Marketing OER
- Instruction
- Collaboration, bringing together a "village" of support
- Budgeting, policymaking, advocacy
- More staff

Q. Briefly describe an example of successful library/faculty collaboration around the initiative?

A department expressed an interest in adapting an appropriate open access textbook for an introductory course. A librarian provided the department with a spreadsheet that identified a variety of open access textbooks on various platforms (OTN, OpenStax, etc.), the authors, and feedback on the potential ease of using each title or platform. Faculty members recognized a specific author's name as an authority in the field; they were thus confident about the quality of his textbook and plan to adapt it.
We have provided workshops introducing OER and have assisted faculty in locating OER for their courses.
The library recently held a two-day "OER Bootcamp" for a faculty member who had received a financial incentive to write an open textbook called *Orientation to Political Science* but needed assistance getting started.
A few faculty have adopted OER for their courses. As a specific example, I promoted an open textbook that Virginia Tech had developed for business courses, and at least one course is using it.
Librarians maintain in-house OER resources through institutional repository software; librarians also guide teaching faculty to external OER resources through regular liaison responsibilities. In turn, faculty regularly revise in-house OER resources, submitting updates to librarians.
We haven't done it yet.
We had one faculty—Political Science—quickly find an open book and adopted that. We had another faculty from Education teaching a children's literature course, where I spent significant time finding licensing information for the children's books. These were not open access, but part of the required readings was from a combination of (1) an open textbook and (2) fair use.
We've had multiple successful collaborations, but one that is longstanding is the collaboration between one of our adjuncts and a librarian. The adjunct teaches a general education science course and has worked closely with one of our librarians for the last two years developing an open pedagogy project where students are creating websites on topics they cover in class. The students openly license these sites and then next semester's students work on revising and building upon it.
We had a faculty learning community built around OER in 2014–15, which resulted in five faculty developing at least one course around OER and/or library-provided online resources.
I am currently working with a theatre professor. She is creating an openly licensed database of Shakespearean monologues. The students are providing the majority of the content. She is providing editorial oversight and I am providing technical oversight.
Successfully transitioned a microbiology course from commercial textbook to a combination of OER and library-licensed content. A faculty member paired with the science librarian to identify useful resources.
As mentioned, our program is just getting started this summer. We have four interested faculty representing Chemistry, Physics, Classics, and History. The Physics professor has already adopted OERs for some of his courses.
Too soon to say. Librarians and instructional technologists are working with faculty this spring and summer.
Instructional designer (library staff) collaborated with a faculty member to create an open pedagogy course and will share developed materials with the OER community.
In 2016, we conducted a year-long OER Faculty Review Program in conjunction with Duke University, Davidson College, and Johnson C. Smith University. We created a LibGuide with links to OER, met with faculty to train them on searching and assessing OER, and required them to select and review 1 large or several small OER resources. Once they submitted their review form, they were given a $250 stipend. Because of limitations in staffing and funding, this program was only offered once and has not been offered again, nor are there plans to do so. Even so, there were several positive outcomes of the project. At Furman University alone, we had one faculty participant create an OER LibreText for use in her class, another faculty member adopt OERs for their class, and a third faculty select the use of OER in Accounting/Finance as a subject of his professional research. He partnered with librarians to conduct research and present his findings.

We are very much in the beginning stages of OER work on campus. However, we are working with the French and Francophone Studies department on converting their entire curriculum to OER. This is currently being piloted via a classroom redesign grant from the Dean of the Faculty's Office.
The Marydean Martin Library at Nevada State College sought to reduce the costs of course materials by designing and leading a six-week open educational resource summer institute for teaching faculty. The rolling impact from the 2018 institute totals approximately $132,000 in annual student savings. During the institute, eight teaching faculty partnered with librarians and other campus stakeholders to convert their core curriculum courses from traditional textbooks to open educational resources. The institute featured sessions on searching for OER, copyright and fair use guidance for the classroom, backward design consultations, Learning Management System (LMS) support, transparent assignment design consultations, and peer review activities.
Librarian and a faculty member collaborated on an OER textbook remix. The faculty member selected materials (librarian helped search) from multiple OER sources and the desired order. The librarian then combined files so the faculty member would have a single PDF file to distribute to students. The course switched from a ~$150 textbook from which only a few chapters were used to a single, free resource that is 100% relevant to the course.
Liaison to the Business and Management department introduced concepts of OER to faculty, who decided they wanted to get as close to providing a textbook-cost-free major as possible. Liaison helped faculty identify texts to adopt across several courses. Faculty members have spoken at OER workshops to colleagues in other departments about their experiences. To date, none of these faculty have applied for the library-funded OER grants. (!)
We've just started the initiative.
No real activity to report.
Again, this is a new program, still underway.
Working group consisting of librarians and faculty created to explore OER program design. Group proposed a grant initiative and funding was confirmed for OER grants for 3 years. Currently, 13 faculty participating in the first phase of the OER grant program.
We found textbooks for freshman-level classes in algebra, biology, and chemistry. A history professor created his own textbook from freely available resources.
Helping to develop a professor's book manuscript into an open textbook.
Developed workshops introducing faculty members to OER creation and resources. These workshops also featured faculty members who have adopted OER sharing their experiences.
Bringing faculty together for lunch to discuss OER opportunities; leading to adoption of an open textbook.
I received a Chancellor's grant to run an affordable course content faculty fellowship to incentivize 7 faculty to adopt low-cost (defined as under $50) or OERs in their courses. We had 19 applications.
We're currently reviewing this process as part of a university task force.
We are just barely getting started. I am currently working with 8 recipients of review stipends and 2 recipients of adoption stipends. Almost every review stipend recipient has told me they hope to actually adopt in the near future. I am planning on having a faculty lunch session in which the stipend recipients will share their experiences.
We have faculty who have adopted open textbooks instead of continuing to use high-priced textbooks.
One of our engineering faculty members developed an online course text to replace his required textbook, which normally costs about $198 (see: https://kdusling.github.io/teaching/Applied-Fluids/Resources.html). Approximately 25 students enroll in his course each semester; with this resource, he saves each class nearly $5,000 in textbook costs.

Our initiative at this point is to raise faculty awareness of OER and encourage OER adoption through an Open Textbook Network membership. This membership will help us reach out to faculty and host OER workshops and training. Success would be further identification of faculty currently using OER and increasing the rate of OER adoption. We have a textbook rental program that is administratively under the library, so we have a good understanding of which faculty are currently using textbooks and have been guiding them through OER options during their textbook adoption process.
Our focus is on affordability rather than OERs or open ed resources. We've approached the affordability piece by matching required course content to library e-book subscriptions and expanded this initiative to purchase required course content as e-books when they are available. We've had great feedback from faculty on how this option has improved access for their students: all students can access e-books in the classroom and can access the e-books from anywhere. We've had a campus event recently in which faculty talked about OER initiatives (OpenStax in Gen Bio and Gen Chem) and a faculty member shared their positive experience in using library e-books in the classroom and offering them as options for students that would like a free copy over purchasing a print copy.
Digital librarian took the lead to transfer and redevelop college readiness class from Blackboard to Moodle; trained faculty with OER digital resources adoption and teaches the class.
Co-requisite, team-taught classes and assignment creation.
This is a work in progress.
Collaboration with the STEM Teacher Education Faculty has introduced future teachers to OER. Through this collaboration, students learned about OER and how to use them in their instruction. In addition, the librarian created a resource guide of OER materials for K-12 education.
Library staff trained faculty on how to use Apple iBooks Author for creating a textbook compiled and designed by students and faculty.
Interactive textbook funded by NEH grant that involved campus faculty, non-local faculty, and a librarian. Librarian provided help with technical and organizational aspects.
For a business ethics course, a librarian consulted closely with the faculty member to identify resources and provide support as the instructor added content to her course site.
We created websites that linked to OER (and other) resources which were added to the courses as supplemental resources or, in many cases, to replace the textbook. Subject matter experts were hired to curate the content which the library team put into the websites, and then the library maintained the websites with the support of curriculum owners. In some cases, faculty teaching the courses also recommended content.
The education library liaison has worked with Education faculty to identify journal articles available in library databases. These articles are used instead of a textbook. The librarian works with the Education faculty to update the article list yearly. Librarians have held training sessions for identifying OER textbooks.
We have had a couple of relatively successful workshops for faculty, but we want to do more. We attended a statewide NJ workshop given by the Open Textbook Network on how to reach and support faculty in doing this (https://vale.njedge.net/event/open-textbook-network-training-workshops/). We created the campus OER Task Force, which is meeting to determine potential funding sources and an action plan. We are working closely with the Student Government Association, some faculty, and staff representatives from the IDC (Instructional Design Center) and ITS (Information Technology Services), so the library would not have to take on those components. We are in the very early stages, but I hope that we see some good progress next academic year (2019–2020) with the plans that the OER Task Force is developing right now. We created a LibGuide for faculty, but right now the OER sources are not listed in our catalog, and we don't have a repository: https://libguides.ramapo.edu/oer. We try to share this on all related Ramapo pages (our library page, IDC, etc.).

Assessed textbook adoptions and identified e-books with unlimited users we had or could acquire and then promoted with faculty. Assisted faculty in finding multiple OER to substitute for a textbook.
The library receives funding from a Title 3 grant for a full-time librarian and coordinates $500 mini-grants; faculty confer with the OER librarian by asking copyright questions, general information on OER materials, and attending library OER faculty workshops.
Reed Library solicited a $25,000 grant from a local foundation to "reduce the cost of textbooks to students." We offered faculty a financial incentive to write an open sourcebook that they would adopt for use in class and make available to others; these books were made available through Open SUNY Textbooks. Reed Library faculty were paid to edit these books. Four books were written: *A Spiral Workbook for Discrete Mathematics* by Harris Kwong, *The Missing Link: An Introduction to Web Development and Programming* by Michael Mendez, *How We Got From There to Here: A Story of Real Analysis* by Robert Rodgers, and *Literature, the Humanities and Humanity* by Theodore Steinberg. Mr. Mendez's book has been downloaded over 200,000 times. Using conservative calculations, this $25,000 grant has resulted in a savings of 2.5 million dollars in student textbook costs.
We currently have two OER initiatives running; for the first, grant funds were used to purchase physical texts to be lent to students, and for the second, the library ran a series of workshops on OER creation, usage, and potential issues for our School of Education. Our user services librarian has collaborated closely with a number of the education faculty to help them create a LibGuide to collocate articles, e-books, and other resources for individual classes. (Obviously, we have taken a fairly broad interpretation of OER for these initiatives.)
Currently, we are working on a plan to adopt OER textbooks for undergraduates and many types of resources for graduate students. We are creating a policy and working with a pilot group of faculty who have chosen to adopt OER resources for fall 2019. There is no money for paying faculty to participate.
One librarian is on the committee of faculty that creates the university published composition guide every year for Freshman Composition I & II.
Faculty participated in a workshop about what open educational resources are and how to find them using Creative Commons and other sites. Pilot faculty then created their site using LibGuides and had that replace the textbook. Student responses were really positive.
We've offered workshops on OER, its challenges, and benefits.
Largely, our OER projects are state-wide university system collaborations spearheaded by the systems University Library Advisory Council, a leadership body of all university library directors. We are currently actively working with a Fine Arts professor on adopting an OER for survey courses.
Several faculty members in the natural sciences and one in the social justice/cultural/travel genre are very adept at constructing study materials. These are subjects that change often with scientific discoveries and social upheaval. Changes occur too rapidly to depend on published works. These professors would rather compile a "course pack" than have students purchase several expensive volumes. We just assist in the search of available current valid material and make suggestions. We also store their course pack after the travel or course. They can revisit them if they want to retrieve something.
Librarians offered OER workshops and led faculty to OER resources, writing OTN textbook reviews, and receiving $200 stipends for their reviews. Librarians and faculty formed an OER committee to draft campus-wide guidelines for faculty using OER and low-cost textbooks. Librarians worked with faculty to heighten their awareness of VIVA course redesign grants. Radford faculty received two grant awards $5,000 and $23,000. Plans are underway to create a modular faculty development program to support. See: https://vivalib.org/c.php?g=836990&p=5978058 for more on the VIVA Open and Affordable Initiatives. Disclosure: I am the current VIVA Steering Committee Chair and have been a part of the VIVA OER Initiatives from the beginning. We were successful in obtaining $600,000 added to the VIVA annual base budget to support OER state-wide in VA.
Assist with writing grants to adopt and/or create OERs.

Faculty members starting a new online master's program worked with librarians to identify OER, OA, and existing library-licensed content to use as course materials.
Here are two: 1. Established an OER Advisory Committee that worked on a campus OER sustainability plan; 2. Planning an OER faculty learning community (FLC) for fall 2019, meeting every other week to take a deeper dive into OER issues, research, best practices, etc. Hoping to write an article about it (OA of course!). Both are currently being led by a scholarly communications librarian.
The library has spent a lot of time helping individual faculty members find materials, often books, articles, e-books, and streaming videos that are part of the collection. Some of our faculty also are not good at adding items to the learning management system (Moodle) and so we have given technical help there as well.
The library director and the director of the Center for Excellence in Teaching and Learning (who is also a biology professor) sponsored a series of 4 workshops this past year to build an OER Learning Community. Each participant received a $200 stipend. Eleven faculty members completed the workshop series. The topics were: (1) Introduction to OER and Goal Setting, (2) Strategies for OER Storage and Distribution, (3) Tools for Revising, Remixing, and Developing OER, and (4) Campus Roundtable: Lessons Learned on OER.
In Texas, there has been a push by the legislature to initiate OER projects (SB 804?), and I was involved in discussions around that legislation at the Texas Council of Academic Libraries (I was on the board in 2017). Since then, Texas has been aggressively looking into OER initiatives, led in part by the Texas Library and Dean Hendrix at UT San Antonio as well as the University of Houston and Texas A&M, and others. Meanwhile, in the summer of 2017, under the leadership of the office of business support services (mail and print shop), they began exploring the possibility of a fee-based rental program (currently $25/credit hour) to cover all textbooks through a P3 partnership with Sodexo. As the committee grew beyond support services, we asked to be included. We have not been. We are expected to "share" information we do uncover on OER and OA initiatives, but we never are included in discussions or given follow up information about decisions. The original program was going to lock in for ten years; somewhere it got reduced to six, I believe. I don't know much more.
The library can provide support in finding authoritative OER and help with copyright questions. It is up to faculty to evaluate the resources and choose how to proceed within their classes with them.
We are in the process of building the program, but one of our librarians chairs a faculty committee under the direction of the Dean of the College's office. This committee is charged with developing a plan for adopting OER resources, particularly focusing on those courses offered as part of the College's General Education program. Ideally, we'd like the program to grow so at least 75% of the GenEd courses are no/low cost to students.
Librarian and a faculty member collaborated to locate an appropriate OER textbook based on the syllabus, of course.
A small grant to replace commercial lab materials with free resources.
Our Business Dept. adopted an open source accounting book. The library worked with faculty to learn more about how OER works and provided potential places to find open source materials.

Q. What are your thoughts on the place of libraries in the future of Open Educational Resources and similar programs?

Libraries have a leadership role in the adoption of OER as part of their contribution to student success and retention. They are at the forefront of advocating for authors' rights and are well-placed to advise faculty on the value of new models of dissemination of scholarly information and research. Additionally, libraries are often the institutional source for copyright information and instruction and thus are poised to address relevant needs with faculty.

Libraries are the perfect place to introduce OER to the world.
Libraries should be at the forefront of the open education movement, but collaboration with campus administration, technical support, and instructional design is critical.
We need to be leading efforts and collaborating with each to offer training and incentives to faculty. VIVA is doing a great job of this. We need more support for staffing. At the local level, we need more support for staffing.
Libraries are a logical place at the university for OER resources to be maintained and curated.
It's critical! Although as a private institution we haven't had administrators realize the actual need from students quite yet. We're eager to get involved, but our administration and faculty are luke-warm.
We hope to reach out to individual faculty to try to encourage interest and participation. I think librarians are perfectly positioned to lead the way in OER initiatives
Our institution has shifted focus to purchasing e-books for the classroom. If an e-book textbook is available, then we get it. The costs for this are borne by our main campus and don't come out of our library budget. And on a mass scale, it is more efficient than the laborious time involved in reshaping course content. The workshops were a mixed success: we had faculty that went with it and worked well with us; then we had others who obviously didn't intend to change anything, liked their convenient way doing things, and just wanted the incentive. Should we do the workshop series again—which we are not planning to at this time—then we need tighter quality control on which faculty participate. That said, I and my librarians are happy and do work with faculty that come to us with these questions, but its more in our liaison role now as a service on demand that we can provide.
Libraries are important partners to promote and adopt OER.
This initiative, though a great idea, are still only a drop in the bucket in cost savings. Someone needs to examine what sort of impact these initiatives have on student retention.
We should be on the front lines; however, there are skill sets that librarians participating in these initiatives will need to grow through professional development. Library leadership will need to realize and support PD for librarians and any support staff involved.
I think it's a need for us to be involved in reaching out to faculty about this, because the students do not have the money to pay for textbooks, and a lot of faculty fail to give us a copy of their textbook to put on reserve.
I believe libraries have a critical role to play, given our focus on access to needed materials for success in college.
Libraries need to be at the forefront of making open educational resources available to their institutions.
I think libraries have long had a role in promoting affordable course materials, and we should look at OER as one of a suite of options (along with course reserves, e-book subscriptions, inclusive access, etc.). It would behoove librarians to be aware of and promote OER in their liaison areas.
Vital and central.
Libraries definitely need a seat at the table. I'm undecided whether that role is one of participant or leader.
Libraries are in the business of connecting patrons with knowledge. OER titles can remove some barriers to access, primarily those related to cost but also barriers from an accessibility standpoint.
Librarians have expertise in finding information and publications, including OERs. Furthermore, we have expertise in creating web directories and tools to help others discover these resources. At Drew, we are also fortunate to have the Instructional Technology group as part of our organization, so instructional designers and LMS admins are serving on the task force and will be direct contributors to the service.
We would be willing to work with professors on listing their resources on the library webpage.

Libraries supply resources and OER fall into that category. It fits easily under the library's umbrella; however, adequate staffing is a major concern.
The library should work in partnership with the dean of the college and dean of faculty for promotion and funding to develop and support an OER program. If those offices are not interested, the library should back away. An OER program must have the full support of those offices to be successful. We took our proposal to the President's Cabinet for adoption as a college priority. Get buy-in from the top before offering a program within the library.
Libraries have a prominent role as facilitators and supporters, but the initiative should be campus-wide.
I don't see that OER promotion and leadership *needs* to come from librarians, but librarians have been the most likely parties to be interested in open resources and have the neutral disciplinary position that makes it possible to work effectively across the campus.
Libraries could be a crucial element in the success of such programs.
We need to be a part of the plans for OER. We can help navigate, organize, and plan for OER on our campuses.
The concept is a great one; however, the choice of open educational resources (textbooks) are very slim in the majority of subject areas. When showing my professors what textbooks are available, they were not impressed with the selection.
As the de facto source for reliable information, it makes sense for libraries to facilitate the identification and assessment of existing OERs and educate faculty/students in their use.
Libraries as service—providing a service for the creation of OER as well as consultants for finding OER.
[With] access to open educational resources, our users, researchers, and faculty may have more opportunities to locate information, always with the collaboration of the librarian.
No comment at this time.
Librarians' expertise and libraries' mission to connect people with appropriate resources are very important to the success of these initiatives. However, libraries and librarians cannot be the only supporting infrastructure (as they currently are at some institutions).
Libraries should provide the infrastructure for OER programs, as we do for all other materials that students and faculty use in courses. What that looks like at each institution may vary as do, for example, our policies on acquiring textbooks for reserve. Libraries should partner with centers for teaching and learning, instructional technology, academic affairs, and student affairs colleagues to help faculty adopt and/or create OER where it makes sense.
I hope that OERs will supplant traditional textbook publishing as the main way to supply students with what they need for coursework.
OER is here and will continue to be. Libraries have always led the way in access, so will continue to do so. This will require changes in librarian skillset and the way the library/librarians are viewed.
Libraries are principally committed to making information and resources accessible to their communities. OERs reduce or eliminate financial barriers that often spring up around academic content. Supporting the development and adoption of Open Educational Resources makes content more accessible, which aligns with the core values of professional librarianship.
Libraries are uniquely situated to instigate and support such efforts; however, it is more difficult at smaller institutions where everyone wears several hats and faculty often are maxed out with course overloads. More progress will probably come from larger institutions, especially if incentives include points toward tenure.
Libraries should play an important campus role in the development and encouragement of OER. Libraries can participate in the OER movement by making OER searchable in the online library catalog, assessing OER use through surveys with students, help faculty find OER, educate the community about open copyright, pursue funding sources for OER, and promote the use of OER as liaisons to departments on campus.

I'm not sure libraries should be spearheading the efforts. I am a firm believer in the programs and the library certainly should be involved, but it seems slightly outside our purview.
A natural development of the libraries' role in encouraging student engagement with information/knowledge and in support of libraries' value of discoverability/accessibility for all. Another arm of what we do—at this point in time, not necessarily replacing other current relevant services. In an academic library, fits into the mission to support faculty teaching and the curriculum and helping faculty as they engage with teaching innovations. Librarians can use for our own purposes in creating OERs that insert information literacy instruction into faculty and student workflows.
Libraries and librarians should partner with faculty on the creation, use, and dissemination of OER. Similarly, when possible, librarians should partner with faculty, staff, and administrators on OE initiatives.
I think that the library has a major responsibility to inform, but I don't know the library should drive this initiative. It is important that the push for OER does not injure pedagogy and innovation. Furthermore, that driving this initiative should be students and textbooks is just a drop in the bucket of college costs. Students should be looking at why the cost of their education is so [high] and how they may combat that issue.
We should be active partners and advocates.
Should be in the lead at their institutions.
I believe libraries are leaders in the field of OER.
Libraries will drive access to these resources, but staff limitations will dictate if the library takes an active role in assisting faculty to develop OERs or makes referrals to external resources like OER Commons, OpenStax, etc.
I think librarians are uniquely positioned to help lead or help build OER initiatives because access to learning materials is a major part of our job(s).
As long as we can continue to financially support faculty, I believe the program will continue to work. We freely acknowledge that open textbooks (OER) create more work for our faculty; it's good if their time can be compensated.
OER can be a powerful way to democratize education. I support the professional work being done on this front, but with a small team (3.25 librarians) and many other campus-related projects underway, we simply do not have the capacity to pursue launching an initiative to foster broader adoption at our institution at this time.
Libraries should continue to provide support for locating and understanding the licensing of open access and open educational resources. However, this movement needs to set down roots in individual departments. Without recognition of open contributions in tenure and promotion policies, even financial incentives will not be enough to sustain and grow open offerings.
Libraries can partner with instructional designers and Centers for Teaching and Learning to explore OER options for faculty and instructors. The library can also help faculty navigate licensing and copyright issues and raise awareness about Creative Commons licensing.
I think there is a place for libraries in the future of OER, but I would say that would be in conjunction with a mix of other solutions for affordable learning initiatives. I don't believe OER is the definitive solution for learning resource affordability.
Honestly, I'd love to shift more of the collection budget to affordability initiatives like what we are doing with library e-books. We're overcommitted to costly journal subscriptions and journal packages and they take up way too much of our budget and limit our abilities to move in different directions—doing our part to address affordability being one. As for OER, I think libraries are going to play a key role in advocating and supporting for OERs. I think there is a role to play in supporting the publishing, sharing, and retention of these resources as they are created on local campuses. We're also looking into software to support our faculty in their OER use. This would allow them to easily remix, customize, include library resources in the content, and sync with the LMS.

Never thought of it but intrigued now that this survey mentions it. Textbook costs are high and the library's textbook on reserve program is well-utilized. Supporting OER makes economic sense for students.
Librarians can definitely help with curriculum and faculty adoption of OER resources by evaluating and measuring the particular resource compatibility with the school/organization's legacy system. Often, libraries are open after hours so the folk's—students—reach out to them for help. Therefore, the library personnel need to know in advance that the programs are being used and given training to be able to support the students.
I think libraries are situated to handle issues regarding open education because they interact with the campus at large and have publishing knowledge and have dealt extensively with fair use practices.
The administration needs to be an important academic partner with the library to help promote and establish OER across campus. It cannot become just a "library thing." Top-down leadership and support are important in any OER endeavor/implementation.
This involves knowledge of resources, organization, and pedagogy. OER becomes an excellent example of academic librarian goals: helping people locate, make sense of, and use information. Librarians are uniquely positioned to become the hub of an OER initiative.
Libraries absolutely have to be a leader/collaborator on these efforts. We can't do it alone, though. Our planning group is comprised of representatives from student government, the bookstore, the office of institutional effectiveness, the library, and faculty.
Librarians are able to assist faculty in locating quality OERs and helping them understand how to appropriately integrate OERs into their courses.
Library publishing, including OER, is becoming increasingly important as we work to guide the creation, discovery, and access to scholarship and educational materials produced in alternative formats and by alternative publishing methods.
I think librarians should play an important part, along with faculty and administration.
I think libraries have a crucial role in conducting outreach about OERs and providing support as faculty seek to transition their courses to OERs. Librarians have experience searching for and evaluating information resources and can familiarize themselves with the landscape of available content so that faculty can turn to them if they are interested in looking into OERs so that they do not become frustrated with the volume and types of offerings online.
OER is as varied as any internet source. Libraries can assist in the search for quality material that fits the need.
If they are financially feasible and do not create legal issues such as copyright infringement, then I am in favor of it.
Go for it.
This is an important campus initiative. Librarians are able to assist faculty members with identifying potential textbooks, understanding copyright, and keeping up to date on developments with OERs.
We hope to be helpful to faculty in locating/assessing/using resources. We could potentially also help with faculty who are interested in creating their own, but I think our focus right now is just on helping to increase the use of OER on our campus.
Good, but way too time consuming to do alone. The lead on our campus was taken by our Center for Information and Digital Literacy. Bigger budget, more staff. We just assist.
Libraries should lead their schools in adopting OER.
I am ambivalent about the role of libraries in OER programs. Resources for higher ed should be chosen for content not cost or format.
Sounds good. We would like to be involved.

Administration is expecting the library to play a role in promoting OER, cataloging faculty created OER, assessment of services, and student feedback.
Librarians are very good at identifying OER materials and materials that can be incorporated into OER publications. Most librarians I have worked with are excellent editors, even of technical concepts that are beyond their training. Financial incentives need to be put in place for the librarians who are participating in OER projects to achieve the best results.
Because of the breadth and depth of resources offered by the library and the basic knowledge of copyright that librarians need to have to function in the field, I feel the library can play a vital role in OER initiatives. The library can function as an informational hub for OER resources and initiatives, providing training, resources, search strategies, publication assistance, and, of course, information literacy for the students using OERs.
I am not familiar with this discussion so really can't comment.
I think it is fine if libraries have the time and resources to pursue such endeavors.
We are the leaders of this initiative and have the skills to carry it through.
Librarians can serve a vital role in selecting and cataloging OERs in OER catalogs (OER Commons, etc.) to make them easier to find. Libraries will likely be the driving force for OER at their institutions because of their unique understanding of the information creation process (finding, storing, organizing, and ensuring proper copyright clearance for information).
I am interested in doing this, it's just that I'm having a hard time now figuring out who on the staff would take the lead on this.
It is the future and how we can really position ourselves to stay relevant.
It will become vital soon.
I think OER is really important and I would love to convince our faculty they should support initiatives designed to use more OER in the classroom. Libraries have to lead the way in using quality OER resources. Not only is it a financial issue (for both schools and students), but it's the future.
We can play a role, but ultimately course content is the responsibility of faculty. At our institution, I have spent more time explaining to faculty what OER is (and is not) than anything else.
The library is the most logical place in the university to spearhead OER programs because of our ability to work across disciplines and departments in the university.
I think libraries and librarians have a great opportunity to assist with this and become an integral part of this worthy movement. We must move on, find new roles. This is another step in our evolution.
Libraries and librarians should play a leadership role in promoting OER across campus and, in our case, across the commonwealth.
Libraries are a natural partner with teaching faculty and others concerned about the high cost of education for our students to promote and encourage the use of OERs.
Librarians are vital to this effort.
To be advocates for OER where appropriate and provide support services as needed
Libraries have a role in helping faculty to understand what open educational resources are and how to find them for possible course adoption. Libraries can have a role in making resources available if they have the financial resources to do so individually or collectively within a consortium.
Since there has been no planning for creating such resources or programs at our institution, I don't have any formed opinions about the topic.
I think library staff can help faculty find materials in their subject and/or work with faculty to provide course packets. I believe that it is still up to the faculty to review material to determine if it is what they want and the information is accurate. However, maybe there could be a nationwide initiative by librarians (ALA, ACRL) to locate and vet materials so faculty will be more amenable to their use. We can also provide a way to organize the materials, and we can help advocate for lower-cost resources for our students.

I do not think that the library should be involved in buying textbooks, whether print or online. However, I am very interested in linking the materials cited in online textbooks to digital and print content in the library.
YES! YES! YES! OER and OA are critical levers for change in the educational landscape. Libraries belong front and center in this discussion. This is a critical time for libraries—embracing OER, OA, open science, and open pedagogy will help libraries stay vital into the future.
Libraries can play a key role in helping faculty identify and utilize appropriate OER resources, many of which are probably already available among library resources.
Instigators, leaders on campus. Facilitators for faculty to learn.
Libraries will support the efforts of faculty in adopting OER. Support will be through information (such as an OER LibGuide). The library will work with the vice president of Academic Affairs Office in planning and coordinating OER workshops, information sessions, etc.
Libraries should help faculty create textbooks or other materials and make faculty aware of library holdings that may serve the curriculum needs. Faculty and administrators often do not understand copyright and librarians should educate on this issue. I have mixed feelings, however, because the administration seems to think that everything is free on the internet. They do not even want to pay consortia fees for repositories. Many of the faculty who have gotten away from textbooks are using library materials such as articles or readings from e-books. The library budget for staff and materials, however, has declined sharply and thus may not be able to support the curriculum as needed.
I think librarians are logical people to help faculty members identify OER and open access materials, and libraries may provide useful repositories of faculty-developed materials in some cases.
If OERs are to be successful, the library has to be part of the solution.
I have favorable views toward these initiatives. They have not been a priority here due to other things that are higher priorities (i.e., open access resources for faculty research), but we do plan to look into Open Educational Resources more closely in the future.
I have mixed feelings about libraries' future with OER. I think we are ideally suited to finding and organizing this information, but I feel broader institutional support is necessary if it is going to be successful. I don't think the library can do it alone.
In all honesty, it depends on the size of the college/university. With only four librarians, we cannot afford to have dedicated staffing/funding for an OER person. I would love to work in a university or mid-sized private college library where we could place more of an emphasis on this.
We are already keeping track of educational resources. This is a natural extension of library services.
OER will become more important as a strategy to lower costs.
Libraries can help to drive the OER movement, but the buy-in has to come from the majority of the teaching faculty. Libraries can assist with finding materials and arranging them for easier access.
They seem to be positioned to take the lead within their institutions to move in this direction.
The biggest stumbling block is copyright restrictions, confusion, and the possibility of stepping on other people's copyright toes. And who on campus will be in charge of tracking it? Small staff, small college, *not* the library if we can help it. Would like to, but the scope would require another librarian and I don't see TPTB funding it.
While we don't have a formal initiative, I *have* promoted the initiative of our statewide library consortium, NCLIVE. It offers grants (which one of our faculty has received) and is aiming toward offering a state OER repository. That said, I see libraries as peripheral to this; we don't have the funding or staff time, and we are not a repository of print textbooks either. I think an OER initiative will have more power if it comes from a provost/dean.
They should take the lead.
Librarians would be very well suited to help faculty find, organize, and ensure access to OERs at an institution.

Integrated into pedagogy design and assessment. It is not exclusively a library issue. While we are involved with promoting resources, it is up to the university faculty to consider adopting open access resources as texts. We can assist them, but they have to be educated and willing, and we can assist with that too.
I think libraries can and should support OER initiatives. In our case, the librarians do not have faculty status, so we do not really have much power to convince faculty to adopt OER, but most librarians think it is a very good idea whose time has come. It is hard to convince faculty that there are good relevant sources out there that are free. We need buy-in from the administration to push faculty to do more with OER. We have very few faculty interested in it here at this time. I think libraries should be at the forefront of making OER resources more available.
It's an opportunity. Librarians have presented to faculty information on OER, along with the advantages and uncertainties, but no follow up on either part.

Q. Please share any additional thoughts you have on OER or affordable course content.

The move toward OER is exciting and timely. Although programs are often driven by cost, benefits include alternative publication opportunities for faculty (whether adopting, adapting, or creating), while students appreciate cost savings as well as ease of access.
We wish our university was ready to provide funding for faculty, but it hasn't happened yet.
I think we (as a movement, not just an institution) need to do a better job promoting non-textbook OERs.
We've got a program called "Ready on Reserve"; we worked with the Office of Diversity and Inclusion. They and we provide funding to purchase texts to put on course reserves, or to just buy the text outright for a student. I think it will soon be a universally expected feature in higher education.
Some formats are more accessible than others. OERs with lots of branding, layers of downloads, and that link to external resources with sketchy copyright still exist and just cause faculty and librarians to say that they don't want to use this. Some format and access models are great, but they don't have content for my liaison area licensed library content should also always be promoted to students and faculty—they're paying for it already, might as well use it.
Library research 1 credit class used OER as course materials.
I think it's important to include affordable course content (particularly library-purchased online resources) in the conversation, not just OER.
Designing course content with OER in mind should be the focus.
I feel that data collection and assessment are currently the most difficult aspects of managing OER initiatives. My place of work is designing a system to make data collection (about faculty OER use) easier, and when that is live, we can hopefully start assessing OER impact more easily.
The "carrot on the stick" for faculty participation is more about whether senior campus administration finds OER of value than the library pushing the initiative.
The high cost of instructional materials is a barrier to student retention and success. By leading OER efforts on our campuses, librarians and technologists make a direct and visible contribution to student success. These projects also build strong partnerships with faculty and academic administrators.
I have a fear that availability would change, so the upkeep of links could become a problem. Also, students have said they still want to hold a print book.
The idea is great, but getting faculty buy-in is an uphill battle. Unless they initiate the conversation, getting them to adapt new materials/processes is really difficult. There are a number of other campus initiatives focused on course materials affordability, one of which is the OER program. Trying to coordinate those initiatives is difficult as each reports up through different VPs …there's no one office that is driving the effort to reduce the cost of textbooks, software, etc.

Even at an institution likes ours, where many students have better financial backing than at other universities, we find that students avoid purchasing textbooks because of cost. OER can be valuable both for its cost savings and for its support of learning outcomes that arise from having immediate and full access to course materials.
My experience is limited except that most of the resources I rely on for course content are public access, full-text material. With students less likely to access materials (even opening a printed textbook after investing in the cost of purchase seems a challenge) making resources available at minimal cost eases one's conscience regarding the cost of materials
It is necessary now. Publishers are getting out of hand with regard to their textbooks, databases, journals, and other resource costs. Faculty also share responsibility by asking the students to purchase the newest edition when an older and cheaper edition would have sufficed. In this day and age of the internet and the multitude of open resources out there made available by other faculty across the world, there is no excuse for not pushing forward with OER.
We need to get more publishers willing to allow OER textbooks to be available (even for a type of flat fee) to make them available to the students
I am concerned about the ephemeral nature of OER websites. In the last year alone, many of the "go to" websites for OER content have shut down or moved locations. It's becoming increasingly challenging to keep links for these resources up to date when they keep disappearing. It also adds to the perception among some faculty that OER aren't "serious publications."
Through the OER, we can librarians identify better resources for the benefit of the programs offered by our faculties of the academic institution. There are many new practices that we can share with the academic community.
No comment at this time.
I wish there were better places to search for OER textbooks in particular. So many people are creating OER now that it's hard to keep up with all the places where they can be found, and not everyone (librarians included) knows where to submit them for discoverability. There is no WorldCat for OER.
Many faculty at Christian institutions of higher education do development of materials that they use to integrate faith and the Christian worldview into their disciplines. This is a ready product with a ready market if the two could find a connection that was easy to implement.
It is an important investment for higher education to help students with cost, but a balance must be developed to avoid violating a faculty member's academic freedom.
Being a small, Catholic school with a high number of first-gen students and students from lower SES families, we're framing it as a social justice issue and that has been pretty well embraced.
We find it a better strategy to focus on Gen Ed/non-major courses.
Anything faculty, librarians, and staff within colleges and universities can do to incorporate affordable course content should be affirmed by the administration. I think institutions whose high-level leadership prioritizes this method of content delivery are more likely to attract and retain students as costs in higher education continue to climb.
We need to be careful about whom we collaborate when it comes to adaptive courseware built around OER. If we are not careful, platforms providers will become the new publishers and we'll face the same predicament which started this whole movement. We need to focus on generating high-quality, peer-reviewed content; leave it to the educators to build the experience around that content.
OER should encourage faculty to explore their approaches to teaching and learning. OER needs to go beyond uploading open course content but encourage students to create and innovate with the materials and get into open pedagogy. The cost of textbooks is a crime. I am interested in anything to help students attending college and to help college more affordable.
At our institution, OER adoption is being driven by individual faculty members.

OER is a much needed "movement" as well as an instructional strategy.
The invisible labor of OER needs to be addressed to ensure that OER is a sustainable model. While it doesn't cost to use materials, these materials must be curated, made sense of, and integrated into teaching.
We just surveyed our students and our faculty (separate surveys). We had 25% response rates for each, so lots of people on campus care enough to weigh in. Faculty really want quality of content. Students want ways to share textbooks.
I think that the creation of a peer review network/credentialing system would be a boost in getting faculty buy-in/ participation.
Not necessarily library related, but I feel a bit uneasy about the lack of compensation for authors in the OER sphere. I am concerned that OER production will become another facet of volunteer service for certain faculty (most likely women, junior and contingent faculty, and students), but better connected faculty (usually men and other senior faculty) will continue to get lucrative contracts with commercial publishers. Some OER authors are compensated, but I have noticed an increase in calls for authors that pay nothing.
I do know some teachers that create their own content such as lecture notes that can be purchased or printed at minimum costs. This seems to work for his students, both academically and financially.
You might want to contact PASCAL, our state consortium to see how all the academic libraries in South Carolina are collaborating. https://pascalsc.libguides.com/scale
Hopefully, they can get good content and a reasonable price.
OER will continue to play a larger role in the mission of the library as time passes.
Commercial textbook publishing is squarely in the hands of big publishers who profit most from the work of authors and editors. It is time for the academy to take back the production and ownership of scholarly content.
I think that finding and updating are key. Also, how do we support faculty who want to publish? Editing and formatting are key and not cheap things to do. Having the things that professors expect these days, like test banks and PowerPoint decks also.
I hope this really develops some traction. I would love to see this take hold at my institution. It would make education much more affordable, distribute research findings faster and allow faculty to tailor their courses. Fingers crossed.
There are many challenges facing OER adoption, including from publishers and campus bookstores. Our OER committee is working with faculty, administration, and bookstore (B&N) to promote OER and low-cost ($40) textbooks. We are also working with the registrar to label courses that have no-cost (OER) or low-cost textbooks. This is part of a state-wide mandate from the VA General Assembly for all public higher ed institutions.
OER textbooks are not enough. We need an open platform for ancillary content.
No additional thoughts.
There are a variety of strategies available to faculty to help make course content affordable. Librarians should encourage faculty to use library-licensed e-books and e-journals as appropriate. Additionally, librarians should educate faculty on finding open educational resources. Libraries should proactively include open access/open educational materials in their discovery tools (discovery layer, electronic journal finders, catalogs, etc.).
Students are the victims of overpriced publications. They need to have access to free or affordable content. Faculty need to be more cognizant of new editions and if they really need them. Maybe a 5th edition is still just as good as a 10th edition, but do they know or are they paying attention? I think it fine for students to pay *reasonable* prices on textbooks. Work has gone into those texts to not only have accurate content but to have ancillary resources, which are hard to find in OER. However, the prices of textbooks are way beyond reasonable. So, I am hoping that we will have an initiative on campus in the near future to start using OER or other similar options.

I would be interested in seeing how OER is affected by visual memory, and to see whether or not student learning is improved by it.
OER is more than making materials affordable and more than a social justice argument about doing the right thing. OER *is* all that and is becoming so much *more*—forcing libraries to re-think services, programs, and resources in new ways to support academic scholarship in humanities, sciences, applied areas, with new collaborative partners and for new purposes. Breaking up publishing monopolies and ensuring commercial interests do not co-opt OER for monetary gain are important to guard against. It will be interesting to see new models emerge. Please keep encouraging librarians to become involved, engaged, and invested. Thank you for doing this important work.
In discussions with other librarians who have OER programs, I think libraries can leverage their influence in assisting with these projects.
OER will gain wider acceptance as the cost of textbooks continues to increase. Also, there is a social justice component to OER, and this aspect supports our mission and university ethos.
I think there is a lot of interest in OER right now, and hopefully some of the useful materials that have been developed to date thanks to major grants will be maintained and updated so they do not lose their relevance and currency.
I'm delighted our university reduced student costs in a way that at least allows for more predictable costs and financial aid support. I don't think rental programs are going to be the final solution. However, the perception (real or intuited) that faculty didn't want to be bothered drove a lot of our decisions. I don't think that is a rare situation in small universities. However, only a truly robust OER, open access model will work long term. Right now, the library is the place to find both OA resources and "free to the student" resources. Why not build on our successes? Lots of higher ed keeps trying to remake the wheel. More collaboration across programs and departments would benefit the students and the long-term health of the institution.
I feel all aspects of the institution need to be on board and not just the library. Administration support is crucial if it is going to succeed. It would also be helpful to have the marketing and fundraising arm of the college involved to help spread the word to prospective students and donors who may be interested in helping get the program off the ground.
It is gaining credibility among our faculty. They are interested, but they haven't done much with it yet. Provost is considering some sort of "incentive" to encourage adoption.
Students are less able to buy course materials as well as less willing. Colleges must make progress to OER.
It seems that is more a question of time rather than interest. Hard to find the extra time to do that one more thing.
Would love affordable course content. I'm sure our students would, too. Do not need the headaches.
The number one reason why students say they don't turn in their work or read the textbook is that they can't afford to buy the textbook.
Emphasize better pedagogy rather than savings.
Sometimes by buying resources that have unlimited use, libraries can also help in this effort. We also can promote open access via our discovery catalogs.
I would be interested to learn about institutional or multi-institutional assessment efforts using OER in courses.

APPENDIX B. RESOURCES FROM SURVEY RESPONDENTS

Connecticut State Colleges and Universities. (n.d.). OpenCSCU. Retrieved from https://cscu.libguides.com/?b=g&d=a

Drew University Libraries. (2020, May). Open educational resources (OERs). Retrieved from http://libguides.drew.edu/OERs

Elon University. (2020, July). Open educational resources (OER). Retrieved from http://elon.libguides.com/oer

Fort Hays State University. (2018). Open textbook grant program. Retrieved from https://www.fhsu.edu/oer/otgp/index

Franklin College. B. F. Hamilton Library. (2019, August). Open educational resources. Retrieved from http://franklincollege.libguides.com/oer

Furman University. Furman Library News. (2017, March 21). Tame wild textbook prices! [Blog post]. Retrieved from http://blogs.furman.edu/library-news/2017/03/21/tame-wild-textbook-prices/

Furman University. James B. Duke Library. (2020, July). Open educational resources (OERs). Retrieved from https://libguides.furman.edu/oer

Hollins University. Wyndham Robertson Library. (n.d.). Open education resources. Retrieved from http://library.hollins.edu/oer/

Lenoir-Rhyne University Libraries. (2020, January). Open educational resources (OERs). Retrieved from http://libguides.lr.edu/oer

Macalester College, DeWitt Wallace Library. (2020, May). Open textbook/OER stipends program policy. Retrieved from https://docs.google.com/document/d/1-bs9rKOLK_Vp5v8dmDOkbry0Bi_gaCri6nNiZQz5tlA/preview

Oswego State University of New York. (2020, April). Open educational resources. Retrieved from https://libraryguides.oswego.edu/oer

Radford University. McConnell Library. (2020, August). OERs: Open educational resources. Retrieved from https://libguides.radford.edu/mcconnell/OER

Saint Martin's University. O'Grady Library. (2020, July). Open educational resources (OERs). Retrieved from http://stmartin.libguides.com/OERs

Saint Xavier University. (2020, September). Open educational resources. Retrieved from https://lib.sxu.edu/friendly.php?s=oer

Susquehanna University. (n.d.). Scholarly commons. Retrieved from https://scholarlycommons.susqu.edu

Susquehanna University. Blough-Weis Library. (2020, August). Open educational resources (OER): OER basics. Retrieved from http://library.susqu.edu/OER

Underwood, T. Furman University. News. (2018, October 9). Taking a bite out of rising textbook costs. Retrieved from https://news.furman.edu/2018/10/09/taking-a-bite-out-of-rising-textbook-costs/

Valley City State University. Allen Memorial Library. (2018, July). Open access. Retrieved from http://libguides.library.vcsu.edu/oa

Valley City State University. Allen Memorial Library. (2019, November). OER: Open educational resources. Retrieved from http://libguides.library.vcsu.edu/oer

Valparaiso University. (2020, September). Open educational resources (OERs): OER development awards. Retrieved from http://libguides.valpo.edu/OER/awards

Valparaiso University. (2020, September). Open educational resources (OERs): What are open educational resources (OERs)? Retrieved from http://libguides.valpo.edu/oer

Western Connecticut State University. Libraries. (2019, November). OER: Open educational resources. Retrieved from http://libguides.wcsu.edu/opened

Wheaton College. Madeline Clark Wallace Library. (n.d.). LTLC funding opportunities. Retrieved from https://wheatoncollege.edu/academics/library/services-for-faculty/funding-opportunities-from-ltlc/

Wheaton College. Madeline Clark Wallace Library. (n.d.). Open educational resources. Retrieved from https://wheatoncollege.edu/academics/library/for-faculty/open-educational-resources/

APPENDIX C. SAMPLE DOCUMENTS

Respondents provided documents and links to a number of resources on their OER initiatives. There were many great resources, and following is a small sampling. The resources and links will provide some examples of guides for finding OER resources, faculty grant programs, details on OER programs, unique OER artifacts, and OER program development. There were many library resource guides submitted that discussed OER in great depth. These contained topics such as OER definition and overview, OER finding guides, OER evaluation links, faculty program information, copyright information, Creative Commons details, videos, PowerPoint presentations, and open access descriptions. Almost all the sites had a series of links to OER resources. These were categorized by either type or subject.

Institution	Sample Documents Provided	Pages
OER Resources Lists		
Elon University Belk Library Elon, NC	• Image of Open Educational Resources (OER) web page. • Link to website.	53
Furman University James B. Duke Library Greenville, SC	• Image of Open Educational Resources (OERs): OERs by Subject web page. • Link to website.	54
Faculty Stipend Programs		
Connecticut College Charles E. Shain Library New London, CT	• Open Educational Resources Grant Program o Rationale o Program Design o Application Categories	55–58
Fort Hays State University Forsyth Library Hays, KS	• Image of Open Textbook Grant Program web page. • Link to website.	59
Macalester College DeWitt Wallace Library Saint Paul, MN	• Open Textbook /OER Faculty Stipends Program Policy o Summary/Background o Levels of Available Stipend Support o Application/Implementation Process	60–64
Oswego State University of New York Penfield Library Oswego, NY	• Image of Open Educational Resources: OER Grant Opportunities web page. • Link to website.	65
Radford University McConnell Library Radford, VA	• VIVA Course Redesign Grant Program o Request for Proposals o Viva Course Redesign Grant Application o VIVA Course Redesign Grant Application Cover Sheet	66–75
Saint Martin's University O'Grady Library Lacey, WA	• OER Adoption Stipend Requirements o Due dates and stipend amounts	76

Institution	Sample Documents Provided	Pages
Western Connecticut State University Haas Library Young Library Danbury, CT	• Image of OER Grants web page. • Link to website.	77
OER Information		
Connecticut State Colleges and Universities (CSCU) Hartford, CT	• Image from website of Create OER: 4 Step Strategy • Link to web page	78
Hollins University Windham Robertson Library Roanoke, VA	• Image of a table showing OER Savings (Spring 2016–Spring 2019) • Link to the image	79
Susquehanna University Blough-Weis Library Selinsgrove, PA	• Image from website of Open Educational Resources (OER): OER Myths • Link to web page	80
University of Findlay Shafer Library Findlay, OH	• Poster: Highlighting Training Sessions Offered	81
Valley City State University Allen Memorial Library Valley City, ND	• Flowchart: Faculty Looking to Implement OER	82
Wheaton College Wallace Library Norton, MA	• Infographic of Open Educational Resources	83
OER Program Development		
Drew University University Library Madison, NJ	• Open Education Resource (OER) Task Force ○ OER Task Force 2019 draft ○ Background/Rationale ○ Recent Initiatives at Drew	84–87
Fort Hays State University Forsyth Library Hays, KS	• Grant Proposal Summary with Funding Structure ○ FHSU Z-Course Grant Proposal Summary ○ FHSU Z-Course Grant Full Proposal	88–93
Furman University James B. Duke Library Greenville, SC	• OER Review Program Overview ○ Summary ○ Background ○ Program Overview ○ Current Status	94–96
Saint Xavier University Robert and Mary Rita Stump Library Chicago, IL	• Image from website of Open Educational Resources: Actions and Explorations • Link to web page	97
State University of New York	• OER Sustainability and Planning Guide	98

OER RESOURCES LISTS

ELON UNIVERSITY

Open Educational Resources (OER)

Elon University's website with OER resources listed by type of resource. http://elon.libguides.com/oer/home

FURMAN UNIVERSITY

Open Educational Resources (OERs): OERs by Subject

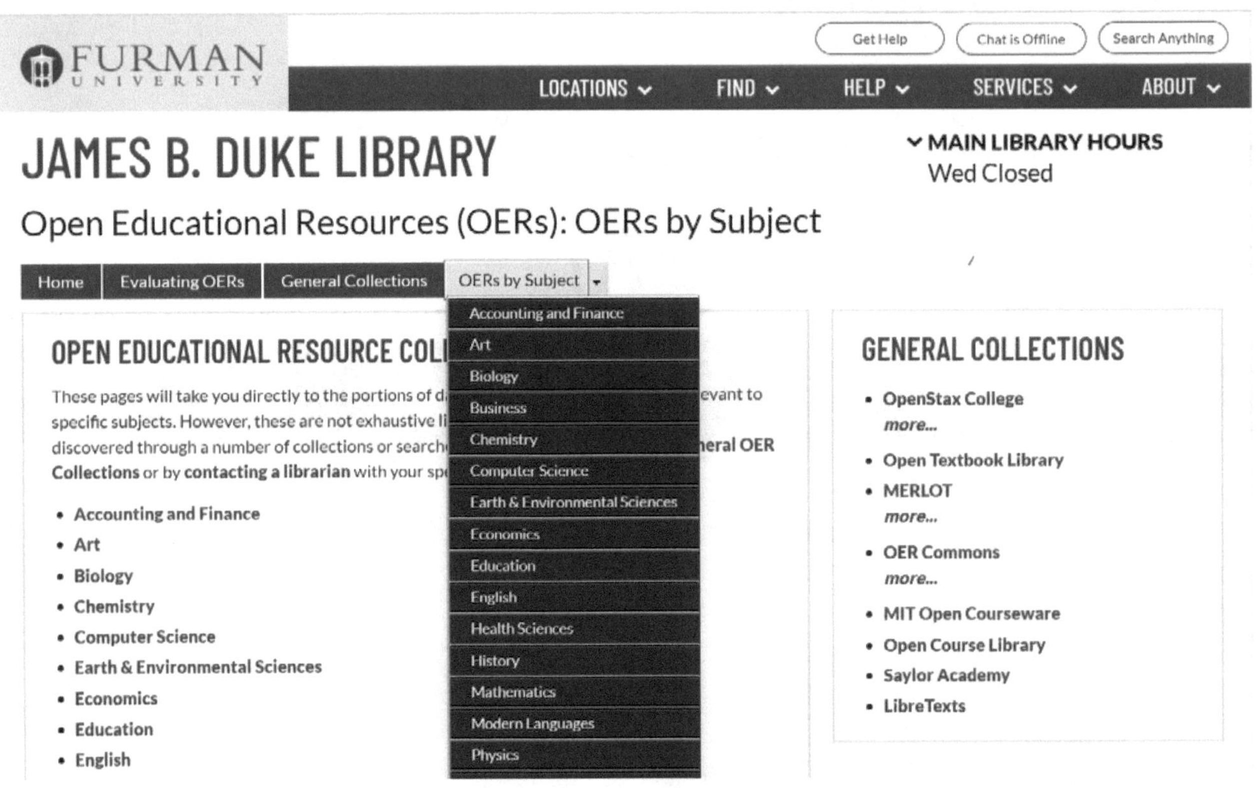

Furman University provides a list of OER resources by Subject. https://libguides.furman.edu/oer/subject

FACULTY STIPEND PROGRAMS

CONNECTICUT COLLEGE

Open Educational Resources Grant Program

Open educational resources (OER) are educational materials distributed at no cost and that have been released under an intellectual property license that permits their free use and repurposing by others. OER include full courses, course materials, modules, textbooks, streaming videos, tests, software, and other materials. For more information see the LibGuide *Open Education Resources at Connecticut College* (https://conncoll.libguides.com/OER).

In order to increase OER course adoptions and encourage faculty exploration and innovation in finding new, better, and less costly ways to deliver quality learning materials to students, the College is providing incentives for faculty to convert courses currently using traditionally purchased materials to use OER material. An OER Grant encourages creation of open educational resources that can be shared widely at the College and with higher-education institutions world-wide.

Rationale

Use of open educational resources will enable students to have access to more dynamic learning tools and a richer academic experience at a cost that will ease the financial burden of our students, encourage full participation and help them thrive academically.

- **Lowering the total cost of education.** The grant aims to reduce educational costs for students by providing free or low-cost learning materials that are available from day one of their classes. The cost of tuition has risen to $69,970 and financial aid spending has increased 3.4 percent at Connecticut College since 2017. In the 2018 New Camel Survey, "almost two-thirds of the class expressed concern about their ability to finance their college education and nearly 70% think that the College should put very much emphasis on addressing students' financial need and concerns." This program will support Connecticut College's strategic priority toward financial strength and exploring new ways to make a Connecticut College education affordable.

- **Improving retention and recruitment, especially among underrepresented groups.** Studies have shown increased student retention and student success using OER. OER improve final grades and increase retention rates for Pell recipient students and underrepresented groups. OER address affordability, completion, and attainment gap concerns.
- **Creating opportunities for pedagogical innovation.** OER and Open Pedagogy are opportunities for pedagogical innovation and improvement. OER can be tailored and improved locally to fit the needs of students, and allows opportunities for student participation in the process of OER creation (Open Pedagogy).
- **Expanding academic freedom.** OER expand academic freedom, giving faculty copyright-free options to produce personalized learning materials to meet the specific needs of our students at our institution. Faculty are untethered from the rigid structures and content produced by publishers.

Program Design

The OER Grant program will provide financial assistance and incentive for faculty to adopt OER materials. An OER Grant is available to all teaching faculty (full-time, part-time, lecturer, and visiting) at Connecticut College. Individuals, teams, Pathways, and departments/programs are encouraged to work together for a unified adoption of OER. Faculty may only receive one grant per course.

Grant recipients must make resources available to a wider audience for several years (i.e., not a one-off, semester project). Participants are expected to emerge as leaders and mentors in the use of OER. Projects will be highlighted on the Open Educational Resources Program page of the College website. In addition, recipients will present their work at a Connecticut College event and will contribute at least one blog post per semester related to their project for the Engage: Teaching with Technology at Connecticut College blog.

Research and technical support will be provided by Information Services to all grant recipients to ensure the successful creation and adoption of OER resources. Recipients will participate in workshops that will cover relevant topics, such as searching for open access material, copyright basics, and integration of OER into Moodle. Regular communication is expected to monitor progress, share information, provide support to one another, and develop community.

A call for proposals will be sent to faculty in early 2019, and notification of awards sent before spring break. Workshops and individual consultation will take place before summer break, and faculty will be expected to work on their courses over the summer. Courses can be taught in the fall or spring semester of the following year.

Application Categories

Grants are administered in two categories: adoption and creation. These categories reflect the differing amount of work for adopting an existing OER textbook versus revising and remixing OER material. Faculty are awarded compensation dependent on the time and effort involved.

Category 1: Adoption and Revision of Existing OER Material

Explore existing open textbooks and OER materials that would be suitable for the course under consideration. Faculty will review materials to ensure they are in line with course outcomes and student success and have the quality and rigor to maintain the integrity of the course. In some cases, existing OER may not be a suitable alternative at that time. Faculty will share the results of their research into OER on the Engage blog.

Selected materials will be used in the course, replacing traditional texts. In addition, faculty may need to revise, remix, or create new supplemental materials suitable for the course under consideration.

- Examples of revision or remixing include editing existing chapters, adding new materials from other sources, removing sections not appropriate, or combining several openly licensed sources.
- Examples of creating new supplemental materials include creating test banks, PowerPoint presentations, videos, images, lectures, and other supplemental materials.

Faculty will receive a $500 stipend for the exploration phase, and an additional $1,000 stipend upon implementation.

Category 2: Creation of New OER Material

Faculty will create new OER material suitable for the course under consideration. Materials must be shared publicly with a Creative Commons license. Applications for category 3 should be developed with library staff to ensure supports are available for the project.

The award for this category is one course remission to offset the significant time required to research, write, and implement new course material.

Criteria

The determination regarding approval of applications and amount awarded shall be made by faculty members of the IS Committee and members of IS staff. Criteria for acceptance includes:

1. Project will reduce student learning costs; proposals with the greatest financial impact will be prioritized.
2. Quality and rigor must be equivalent to existing texts used in courses.
3. Contributes to innovations in college curricular activities.
4. Results in creation and public distribution of open educational resource(s).
5. Aligns with current academic initiatives and priorities, and is coordinated with efforts across the College, discipline, or program.
6. Information Services staff and resources can reasonably support proposed projects.

Proposed Budget

Annual budget will depend on number of grants awarded, not to exceed:

Adoption and Revision Grants (Exploration)	$2,000
Adoption and Revision Grants (Implementation)	$3,000
Creation Grant (in form of Course Remission)	$5,800
Travel or guest speaker	$1,000
Software/ Subscriptions	$600
Food for meetings	$150
Total	$12,550

FORT HAYS STATE UNIVERSITY

Open Textbook Grant Program

Fort Hays State University's Open Textbook Grant Program
https://www.fhsu.edu/oer/otgp/index

MACALESTER COLLEGE

Open Textbook/OER Faculty Stipends Program Policy*

Note: This program is administered by the DeWitt Wallace Library. Please contact us at scholarpub@macalester.edu with questions about this program.

Open Textbook/OER Faculty Stipend program application form.

Summary/Background

College textbooks have increasingly come under scrutiny. Faculty voice concerns that existing commercial textbooks do not always meet the changing needs of their classrooms and teaching methodologies. Open textbooks are frequently identified as a solution to this issue. This program was established to help faculty adapt/adopt/create their own open textbooks.

A key resource of the Open Textbook Network is the Open Textbook Library, the leading discovery tool promoting access to existing peer-reviewed open textbooks. The Open Textbook Library includes freely available, openly licensed, fully complete textbooks. Joining this network is another effort made by library staff to promote the use of open access programs and to provide access to the high-quality resources needed to support the scholarship and teaching at Macalester College. Textbooks produced as part of our program will be made available in the Open Textbook Library.

Program Goals

The goals of the Library's Open Textbook/OER Faculty Stipend Program are:

1. to help eliminate barriers to adapting and/or creating open textbooks and open educational resources on campus by providing start-up funding and other support resources to faculty;
2. to encourage faculty experimentation with open educational resources that can be customized to their specific classroom needs;
3. to help counter rising textbook costs and the potential negative impact that this trend has on student access to classroom learning resources and, therefore, on student success;
4. to contribute to the general availability of high-quality open educational resources.

* *Open Textbook/OER Faculty Stipends Program Policy*, 2018, revised 2021, by the Macalester DeWitt Wallace Library

Levels of Available Stipend Support

Stipends vary in funding levels based on whether an open textbook is being adapted or created. Submitting an application does not guarantee approval of funding. Projects will be accepted for funding until funds are no longer available. Stipend funds may be limited.

General funding guidelines are provided below:

LEVEL #1: Adapting an existing open textbook/OER for use in a course

(Eligible for stipend of $300 per textbook project)

This stipend level is intended to support faculty who are interested in identifying and adapting an existing open textbook or supplemental resources that requires limited revisions, changes or additions.

Examples of minor revisions would be:

- rearranging existing content within a selected open textbook, and/or
- identifying existing supplemental resources to use with an existing open textbook

LEVEL #2: Creating a new Open Textbook/OER for use in a course

(Eligible for stipend of $1,200 per textbook project)

This stipend level is intended to support faculty who are interested in creating an open textbook or suite of supplemental resources that would involve the creation of significant original materials.

Examples of the creation of an open textbook/OER would involve:

- authoring original content for an open textbook with potentially the addition of some content from existing open textbook resources,
- authoring a combination of supplemental resources (slide sets, quizzes, lesson plans, teaching notes, etc.) to use with a remixed/newly created open textbook, and
- mixing substantial content from multiple open textbook resources and supplemental resources to create a newly adapted work.

Faculty may identify open textbook resources for adapting using the Open Textbook Library or any available resource that identifies open textbooks. See the *Library Guide on Open Textbooks* for more information. Contact scholarpub@macalester.edu with questions.

Some examples of how funds can be spent/used include the following:

- Software costs*
- Platform expenses
- Editing/proofreading
- Layout/design
- Hiring student assistants

If you have specific questions on spending limitations of program funds, please contact us.

*While commercial/licensed proprietary software can be used in the creation of an open textbook covered by this stipend, it is not acceptable to require the use of commercial/licensed proprietary software in the ongoing use of the completed open educational resource.

Eligibility for Funding

To be eligible under this program, the open textbook/OER proposal must meet program eligibility requirements. These are:

1. The applicant must be an instructor teaching courses at Macalester College during the academic year in which funding is provided. Tenured, tenure-track, or NTT series are given highest priority. If other contributors are included, such as students, non-instructional collaborators (lab managers, native speakers, etc.) or instructors from other educational institutions, it is the responsibility of the applicant to determine what, if any, fund sharing is appropriate and to coordinate this directly. Be aware that funds under this program will be dispersed as a transfer into the faculty applicant's FTR account(s).
2. Open textbooks and open educational resources being adapted/created for ongoing courses will be considered for program funding. Ongoing courses are defined as courses included in the routine course offerings for a department and listed in the College catalog (for example, a course offered every spring semester).
3. All open textbook creations/revisions and accompanying supplementary materials resulting from the Open Textbook Faculty Stipend Program must be made available through the Macalester College *Digital Commons* repository under a Creative Commons license. The faculty author retains copyright of the work. The library will also submit the completed textbook to be linked from the Open Textbook Network's Open Textbook Library, a leading index of open textbooks.
4. Open textbooks and open educational resources created or adapted with funding from this program should *replace* the traditionally published textbooks or resources in the courses for which they are prepared. No funding will be provided for open textbooks already in use as the primary textbook for a Macalester course unless some original authoring, either through revision of the existing open textbook is done or accompanying supplementary materials that add value to the original text are created. Original supplementary materials may include, but are not limited to, problem sets and answer keys, test and quiz questions, slide sets, videos, lesson plans, teaching notes, and/or detailed study guides.
5. As we seek to impact the largest number of students possible and have the highest financial impact possible, priority for approved projects will be given to proposals for open textbooks which will be used in courses that are already part of the MCSG Reserve Textbook initiative. This MCSG initiative targets relatively expensive textbooks and textbooks that the most students use on campus.

Application/Implementation Process

Open Textbook Faculty Stipends are available through an ongoing application process that is competitive. Faculty submit their request for funding using the Open Textbook Faculty Stipend program application form. Applications for stipends will be accepted beginning June 1 for the academic year starting that fall, and they will be reviewed as submitted. Applications will be received and considered on an ongoing basis as long as adequate program funds remain available.

Applications are reviewed by a committee of library staff. Current committee members for academic year 2020–2021 are Beth Hillemann, Research & Instruction Librarian for Social Sciences; Louann Terveer, Digital Initiatives Librarian; and Jacki Betsworth, Senior Library Specialist.

Initial funding for approved projects will be made available within 30 days of approval, and will be deposited in faculty applicant's FTR account. Half of the funds are made available at the start of the project with the balance being made available once the textbook project is completed unless other arrangements are approved. If a faculty member is unable to meet the terms of the agreement with the library, the individual will forfeit any remaining stipend funds.

Projects approved through this program involving the *adaption* of an existing open textbook/OER are expected to be completed and in use no later than two (2) full semesters after initial funding is received or the next time the course is offered after that.

For projects involving the *creation* of an open textbook/OER, the textbook is expected to be completed and in use no later than three (3) full semester after initial funding is received or the next time the course is offered after that.

Requirements for Projects Approved for Funding

1. Initial Consultation Session
   Library and ITS staff can help you discover open textbooks suitable for adaption or other open content, can respond to Creative Commons licensing and copyright issues, and can help brainstorm technology issues related to your project. An initial consultation with librarians is expected of each proposal that is approved. Library/ITS staff will remain available to assist and provide support throughout the entire project.
2. Progress Reports
   Successful applicants should provide a timeline for their project that includes at least two progress updates, one at two months after initial funds are received and the other at six months. This project update can consist of a brief check-in session with Louann Terveer or a brief written report.
3. Peer Review of Textbook Project
   Textbook projects that are created using funds from this program will be expected to go through a peer-review process. Library staff are currently developing this process in collaboration with faculty members and subject librarians from established networks such as the Oberlin Group of libraries and the Open Textbook Network.
4. Assessment Activities
   Successful applicants are expected to collaborate with library staff on assessing the impact of open textbook resources that result from stipend funding. Library staff will initiate and help facilitate these efforts. Assessment involves reporting to the OTN and SPARC on the number of students using the open textbook and cost savings that result from the use of the textbook. An additional impact factor will be the faculty member's assessment of successful use and acceptance by students enrolled in the course.
5. Change in Publishing Plan

If a faculty member contracts with a commercial publisher, and this results in the funded textbook not being openly accessible and reusable (i.e., having cost or access barriers and/or restricted use licensing), the faculty member will forfeit any remaining stipend funds and must return any funds previously received.

OSWEGO STATE UNIVERSITY OF NEW YORK

Open Educational Resources

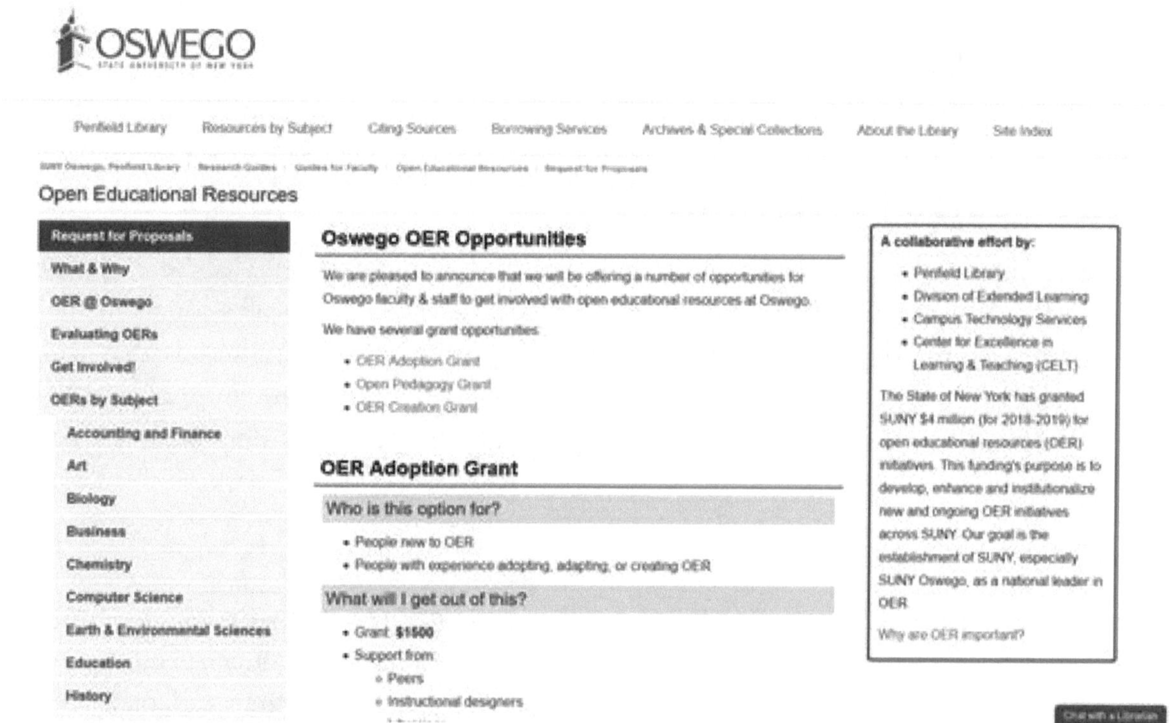

Oswego State University of New York has three different faculty grants available to their faculty. https://libraryguides.oswego.edu/oer

RADFORD UNIVERSITY

VIVA Course Redesign Grant Program

Request for Proposals

The Virtual Library of Virginia (VIVA) requests proposals for its 2019 Course Redesign Grant Program. VIVA Course Redesign Grants are awarded to educational professionals in the state of Virginia who wish to adopt, adapt, or create open or no-cost course materials that will greatly reduce the cost of those materials for students in courses in any discipline. Applications that foster multi-institutional efforts are encouraged. All applications are due September 30, 2019.

Grant Purpose

The Virginia General Assembly has provided funds to support the Course Redesign Grant Program through VIVA (https://vivalib.org/viva/homepage/), a program of the State Council of Higher Education. This grant program focuses on reducing the costs of higher education for Virginia students by eliminating textbook costs. Textbook costs can be a significant barrier to student success, shaping everything from what majors are chosen to whether or not degrees are completed. The high cost of textbooks, currently estimated by The College Board to be around $1,300 per student per year, means that students often do not purchase course materials, and their academic performance suffers as a result.

Although the need is clear, faculty who wish to redesign courses using open or no-cost materials have little resources and time made available to them for these efforts. The purpose of the Course Redesign Grant Program is to acknowledge and provide support for the time and effort it takes faculty and professional staff to redesign courses using open or no-cost materials, and to empower Virginia educators to contribute to the field of open educational materials. Grants are intended to:

- Support a variety of approaches for course redesign using resources that are free to the student, such as Open Educational Resources (OER) and/or available online library resources, including adoption, adaptation, and creation of OER and/or identification and adoption of materials already available to VIVA institutions through their libraries.*
- Provide support to faculty, libraries, and their institutions to implement these approaches.

---

* A librarian or project manager can help guide faculty to appropriate library materials. If the course would continue to require costs to students such as for homework software or coursepacks after the grant work is complete, applicants must detail how open or library materials do not currently exist that could meet this need and/or how they are planning future grants to meet this need.

- Lower the cost of higher education for Virginia students and contribute to their retention, progression, and completion.

Grants are meant to preserve academic freedom and provide both incentives and support to this critical work. The funding model is based on other statewide models, with particular thanks to Affordable Learning Georgia.

Grant Guidelines

Full or part-time faculty may apply for a grant to support the adoption of OER, including textbooks, software, and library resources that replace a traditional textbook, or a combination of OER and library resources. Grants will be awarded from $1,000–$30,000 and are designed to support faculty members in transitioning to course materials available at no cost to students. Proposals may involve one person or teams of any of the following: teaching faculty, librarians, instructional designers, subject matter experts, editors, graphic designers, or others as needed. While individuals can be involved in more than one applying team, they may not be listed as the Primary Investigator (PI) in more than one proposal, nor may they be the PI on more than one grant simultaneously, including grants awarded in previous years.

Applications will be reviewed by members of VIVA's Open and Affordable Course Content Committee, VIVA administrators, and peer-reviewers. Grants will be awarded based on:

- potential for student savings, including class enrollment and cost of existing course materials
- the use of OER (freely available and free to be modified)
- frequency of course offering, with a preference for high enrollment, required courses, and/or courses that are part of the SCHEV Passport Program[†]
- impact of the project on open education, such as the development of high-quality resources in areas for which minimal open content is currently available
- a preference for multi-institutional efforts with broad statewide impact
- commitment to adopt/adapt/create course material for a course scheduled for no later than spring semester, 2022.
- commitment to continue offering the course materials to students at no cost for future semesters/years[‡]
- agreement to the terms of the grant and required activities

Grant Type Classifications

Proposals that are awarded a Course Redesign Grant will fall into one of three grant type classifications.

† At the time of this proposal's writing, these courses were: Communication (ENG 111), Humanities/Fine Arts (ART 101, ART 102, ART 201, ART 202), Social/Behavioral Science (ECO 201, HIS 111, HIS 112, HIS 121, HIS 122, PLS 135, PLS 211, PSY 200, SOC 211), Natural Sciences (BIO 101, CHM 101, CHM 111), and Mathematics (MTH 154, MTH 155, MTH 161, MTH 167, MTH 245, MTH 263).

‡ For courses that have any remaining costs to the student, applicants must detail how open or library materials do not currently exist that could meet this need and/or how they are planning future grants to meet this need.

- Adopt: Those who "adopt" a resource will be using existing resource(s) as-is or with minimal editorial changes.
- Adapt: Those who "adapt" will be modifying resource(s), combining several existing resources with changes, or creating ancillaries for an existing resource. This includes projects in which curation or pre-existing material results in the creation of a new resource.
- Create: Those who "create" OER will be creating the resource all or largely from scratch.

Grant Funding Categories

There are two grant funding categories: standard-scale (with a maximum award of $10,000) and large-scale (with a maximum award of $30,000). Funding depends on the size of the team and impact of the project, as outlined below. VIVA will pay travel costs (within George Mason University travel reimbursement policy) for one to two team members to a required, central kickoff meeting for the program.

Type	Description	Examples
Standard-Scale	Typically for smaller teams at individual institutions. Almost always for grants that fall under adoption and adaptation classification, rather than creation. Awards up to $10,000. Typical team member limits of $1,000 (adoption), $2,000 (basic adaptation or creation of ancillaries such as question banks or lecture slides), or $3,000 (significant revision or remixing). $5,000 maximum per team member.	Adopt: Redesign your STAT 203 course, making use of OpenStax Statistics as the textbook without making changes to the content. Basic Adaptation: Redesign your BUS 220 course, making use of Focusing on Organization Change and incorporating industry case studies from other OER. Ancillaries: Redesign your SOC 320 course, creating quiz questions for Principles of Sociological Inquiry. Revise/Remix: Redesign your COMP 150 course, making use of Database Design, significantly revising each chapter to include new software features, and writing new chapters to cover learning objectives for your course not found in other OER.
Large-Scale	The project must demonstrate large-scale impact through high-enrollment, broad change (such as a department-wide transformation or affecting multiple institutions), or content creation for a discipline and level of study not currently covered by existing open materials. Awards range from $10,000–$30,000. $5,000 maximum per team member. Large-scale grants must designate a project manager.	Broad Impact: Redesign all sections of the PSYC 100 course offered at three partner institutions. Creation: Redesign your BIO 450 course, creating a substantially new open textbook or open course where it is possible to demonstrate that quality open resources are not currently available.

Each awarded grant will receive a project orientation at a kickoff meeting and ongoing support from VIVA staff, including Creative Commons license support. Adapt and Create grants will also receive support in modifying existing OER, access to Pressbooks, copyright consultations, DOIs, and ISBNs, where needed. All created or modified material resulting from these grants must be in a format that can be hosted on a shared repository platform by VIVA, and VIVA requires permission to host the content in perpetuity. In addition, grant recipients will be expected to participate in the following required activities:

- Institutional sign-off on a Memorandum of Understanding (MOU) provided by the VIVA Central Office, using the project proposal as a statement of work.
- Attendance by at least one team member at a required kickoff meeting.
- Project Managers and PIs must meet virtually once at the outset of the project with the VIVA Open and Sustainable Learning Coordinator.
- Completion of a project status report for every semester of the implementation.
- Completion of all textbook and resource creation/adaptation and course redesign as described in the statement of work.
- Completion of a final project report, including provision of data on impact on student success and a course syllabus with resource links. The report must include overall changes in Drop/Fail/Withdraw (DFW) rates and student performance (examples: grades, standardized tests, other learning outcomes assessments).
- New works must be created under a Creative Commons Attribution License (CC-BY), with exceptions for modifications of materials with a more restrictive open license, and will be made accessible to the public through the VIVA shared repository platform. This requirement does not include proprietary features of authoring platforms. If works developed in authoring platforms have proprietary features that are unable to be accommodated in the VIVA shared repository, such as particular test bank structures that are platform-dependent, applicants should include plans for how that content can be shared.
- A spreadsheet or record of the copyright status of all incorporated material, including text, images, video, and music/sound files.
- Content created is owned by the creator, but VIVA requires permission to host the content in perpetuity.
- Participation as needed in VIVA-related communications, including post-project surveys.

Timeline

- June 10–September 30, 2019: Applications submitted
- September 30, 2019: Deadline for applications
- October 1–December 8, 2019: Application Review
- December 9, 2019: Notification Date
- February 21, 2020: Kickoff Meeting in Richmond, VA

Course materials must be piloted by spring semester, 2022.

Funding Details

Course Redesign Grants differ substantially from federal or other external grants. They are an allocation of state funds through the VIVA program. This funding structure, facilitated by an MOU, allows for flexibility between institutions. Funding procedures largely rely on the policies of the institution with which the project's PI is affiliated, as long as spending meets state guidelines. The proposing team must coordinate as necessary with their Grants, Research, and/or Business Offices per institutional guidelines to determine how to handle the distribution. **Course Redesign Grants cannot cover indirect costs, as they are not external grants.**

Funds can cover faculty and staff time and compensation, including course release time, overload pay, and replacement coverage, depending on institutional and departmental policies. Both faculty and professional staff on awarded teams should qualify for compensation or release time for their work on a project, subject to institutional guidelines. Students can be involved in working on aspects of the project as employees or as part of their coursework. Funds can also cover common project expenses, including design and administrative support. Food, publication fees, professional memberships, software, and hardware are not usually funded; requests for funds in these categories must be specifically justified in the project proposal. In addition, conference travel will be capped at $1,000.00 per person for no more than two people per grant. Grant recipients will have access to Pressbooks and should not include funds for a Pressbooks instance in their budget.

Funding will be released to the sponsoring institutional office in two parts: 75% on return of the VIVA-drafted MOU with the original or modified proposal serving as the statement of work, and 25% on submission of the final report.

VIVA will pay travel costs (within the George Mason University travel reimbursement policy) for one to two team members to a required, central kickoff meeting for the program.

PIs will be responsible for communications between VIVA and their institutions regarding funding.

Webinars for Review

Webinars will be held for a general introduction to the application process and Q&A:

- Wednesday, July 10, 10–11 am
- Thursday, August 29, 11 am–12 pm
- Thursday, September 26, 1–2 pm

Viva Course Redesign Grant Application

The VIVA Course Redesign Grant Program focuses on reducing the costs of higher education for Virginia students by eliminating the costs of textbooks and other course materials, providing faculty and staff with the resources to produce pedagogically advantageous course materials, and empowering Virginia educational professionals to contribute to the growing field of open educational resources (OER). To apply for a VIVA Course Redesign Grant, please submit a proposal that describes a project that will adopt, adapt, or create an open or no-cost resource. Proposals should include the following components:

1. A cover sheet (please use included cover sheet template)
2. Project Information
3. A narrative description of the project that includes the following sections:
    a. Project Goals
    b. Impact Statement
    c. Action Plan
    d. Quantitative and Qualitative Measures
4. Timeline
5. Budget
6. Sustainability Plan
7. Statement(s) of Support

Each project should use the attached institutional support template to include a signed statement of support from the Primary Investigator's (PI) affiliated department or college (not the affiliated Office of Sponsored Programs). A statement of institutional support must be signed by a person administratively above the PI or team member. Two additional, contextual letters of support from the field will be accepted. More than two additional letters will not be forwarded to the committee.

The application should not exceed 10 pages in length (including the cover page but not including the letters), and should be submitted as a single Word document by midnight on September 30, 2019, via email to viva@gmu.edu.

Instructions

A. Cover Sheet (one page maximum)

Each application should use the included template to attach a one-page cover sheet to their application. The cover sheet includes the following information:

- PI Name (with appropriate title, Dr./Ms./Mr./Mx.)
- Institution and Department
- Address
- Email Address
- Phone Number
- Name and contact information of departmental administrator for accounting/budget management
- Title of project
- Semester alternative textbook/course materials will first be implemented
- The type of grant category that best fits your project (Adopt/Adapt/Create—Select only one)
- Amount requested
- Abstract of project (150 word maximum)

B. Project Information

Project Information should include:

1. The name, institution, email address, and a brief bio (maximum 150 words) of all team members. Large scale projects (those over $10,000) must identify a project manager. You should also indicate which team members (up to two) will be available to attend the kickoff meeting in Richmond on February 21, 2020.
2. Course Information including:
    a. Class prefix and number (e.g. PHIL 1113)
    b. Title of class (e.g. Introduction to Logic)
    c. Catalog description
    d. Please provide a summary of the schedule of this course and its instructors. The summary should include: how often the course is taught, how frequently the applicant teaches it, the number of total sections offered, number of students per section, and how often this resource will be used in this class. Please include other instructors' names who will be using this resource.
    e. Number of students who will use this resource the first semester offered
    f. Total annual number of students who will use this resource in subsequent academic years by instructors who have committed to its adoption

    If the resource will be used at multiple institutions, include the above information for each institution.
3. Resource(s) Being Replaced, for each include:
    a. Title
    b. Author(s)
    c. ISBN
    d. Retail cost ("new" price from Amazon)
    e. Amazon.com link to resource
4. Calculated Virginia Savings Per Academic Year:
    a. Original Total Cost per Student (all resources together)
    b. Projected Total Annual Virginia Student Savings Per Academic Year (total number of students per year in courses taught in Virginia committed to adopting the resource multiplied by the original total cost per student)
5. Resource(s) Selected:
    Please discuss in detail the materials that will be used to replace a traditional textbook, including how students will access the content. If students will be accessing content via proprietary software (for example, Canvas), include a detailed description of how this content will be made available to others beyond the PI's institution, as well as how it will be made available in the VIVA repository.

C. Narrative Description

The Narrative section should include a substantive, specific description of the project, with particular attention paid to available OER that will be adapted or adopted, what the final product will look like, how students will access the resource, and any plans for encouraging wider adoption throughout the state. The following sections should be included:

1. Project Goals. Goals for a Course Redesign Grant project go beyond just cost savings. Include goals for student savings, student success, materials creation, and pedagogical transformation.
2. Impact Statement. Course Redesign Grants are awarded to teams and individuals focused on creating significant changes. This section allows teams to describe why the project should be awarded, including an overall description of the project and how it will impact the course, department, and institution.
3. Action Plan. Course Redesign Grant projects can be work-intensive and require project management in order to be successful. This section allows teams to describe how the team will fulfill the goals of the project. Include the following:
    - The activities expected from each team member and their role(s): subject matter experts, instructional designer, librarian, instructor of record, project manager, etc.
    - The identification, review, selection, and adoption/adaptation/creation of the new course materials that are necessary to redesign the course. (A fully prepared application should include a summary and brief evaluation of currently existing OER for adoption or modification or library materials, and/or a preliminary plan to create new materials.)
    - Any additional redesign work necessary for the transformation. (Instructional design, curriculum alignment, accessibility, etc.)
    - The plan for providing access to the new materials to your students and to those throughout the state. (The VIVA shared repository platform can host any adapted or newly created materials. Indicate if you are using other platforms in addition to the repository.)
4. Quantitative and Qualitative Measures. All Course Redesign Grant projects must measure student satisfaction, student performance, and course-level retention (drop/fail/withdraw rates), but teams and institutions may do this in a variety of ways. Outstanding applications will include measures beyond the minimum that enable additional meaningful insights into the impact of the project. Include the following:
    - The quantitative or qualitative measures to be used, along with a description of the methods and/or tools used to gather and analyze data.
    - If the team needs IRB (Institutional Review Board) approval, please indicate this here. Each institution's IRB functions differently and teams will need to know how their institution's IRB evaluates and approves of institutional research.

D. Timeline

This section allows teams to describe how the project will progress from its inception to the final report (submitted at the end of the final semester of the project). Please provide a list of major milestones for the project here.

E. Budget

Include overall personnel and projected expenses. Funds can cover faculty and staff time and compensation, including course release time, overload pay, and replacement coverage, depending on institutional and departmental policies. Both faculty and professional staff on awarded teams should qualify for compensation or release time for their work on a project, subject to institutional guidelines. Students can be involved in working on aspects of the project as employees or as part of their coursework. Funds can also cover common project expenses, including design and administrative support. Food, publication fees, professional memberships, and hardware and software are not usually funded; requests for funds in these categories must be specifically justified in the project proposal. In addition, conference travel will be capped at $1,000.00 per person for no more than two people per grant. Course Redesign Grants cannot cover indirect costs, as they are not external grants. Grant recipients will have access to Pressbooks and should not include funds for a Pressbooks instance in their budget.

F. Sustainability Plan

Course Redesign Grants should have a lasting impact on the course for years to come. In order for this to happen, a Sustainability Plan needs to be in place after the end of the project. Please include here your plans for offering the course in the future, including:

- The maintenance and updating of course materials
- Any possible expansion of the project to more course sections in the future
- Future plans for sharing this work with others through presentations, articles, or other scholarly activities

G. Letters of Support

Letters of support should be submitted with the application as separate pdf files. They do not count toward the application's ten-page limit.

Institutional Letter of Support

Each affiliated department or college should include the following statement of support on letterhead and signed by a person administratively above the Primary Investigator (PI) or team member:

> To the VIVA Course Redesign Grant Committee:
>
> I write on behalf of (Affiliated Professional) in support of their proposal entitled, (Name of Grant Proposal). The (Name of Department or College) strongly supports this effort and is willing to comply with the terms of the grant as outlined in the request for proposals released in June, 2019. This includes, but is not limited to, supporting the implementation of the curricular resources adopted/adapted/created by this project in the classroom and reporting data on their impact on student success.
>
> Signed,
>
> (Name of Department Head)

Any additional language or statement should be reserved for a contextual letter of support as described below.

Contextual Letters of Support (not required)

You may include up to two contextual letters of support for your proposed project from a disciplinary society, open organization, or other professional organization that speaks to the need for development of open materials in this subject area.

VIVA Course Redesign Grant Application Cover Sheet

Contact Information

- PI Name (with preferred title, Dr./Ms./Mr./Mx.):
- Institution and Department:
- Address:
- Email Address:
- Phone Number:
- Name and Email Address of Departmental Administrator for Accounting/Budget:

Project Information

Project title: ______________________________

Semester project will first be implemented: ______________________________

Grant category (Adopt/Adapt/Create; please select only one): ______________________________

Amount requested: ______________________________

Project Abstract (150 words maximum): ______________________________

SAINT MARTIN'S UNIVERSITY

OER Adoption Stipend Requirements

This $750 stipend has been created to encourage faculty to adopt/adapt an OER for use in a course. This stipend is available for both tenure-track and adjunct faculty members.

The stipend recipient will be required to do the following:

By June 15, 2019, $250

- Set up a consult with the Information Literacy Librarian to discuss the adoption process and conduct a preliminary search.
- Select a usable textbook.
- Provide an initial statement that includes the following:

1. Tell what textbook you will be replacing and a brief statement on your use of it in the past (when you selected it, strengths and weaknesses, student reaction, etc.).
2. Tell what your criteria for selecting an open textbook is—you may want to consider the Open Textbook Library review criteria to help guide your evaluation of the resource (https://open.umn.edu/opentextbooks/reviews/rubric).
3. Include your thoughts/predictions on how adopting an OER could affect your course design (we are interested in learning about how adopting OER affects workflow and course planning.).
4. Include an estimated cost savings for students based on projected enrollment.

By September 15, 2019 (if adopting for fall 2019) or February 3, 2020 (if adopting for spring 2020), $250

- Provide a copy of the syllabus.
- Provide a brief statement on how the selection affected your course design, readings, assignments, etc.

By January 15, 2020 (if adopting for fall 2019) or June 15, 2020 (if adopting for spring 2020), $250

- Provide a brief report on your experience using an OER that includes the following:
    1. Tell how using an OER actually affected how your class ran—readings, discussion, etc.
    2. Tell how using an OER affected student learning/success.
    3. Give an estimated cost savings for students, based on actual enrollment.
    4. Include a reflective statement on your experience, including "lessons" for others interested in using OERs.

WESTERN CONNECTICUT STATE UNIVERSITY

OER Grants

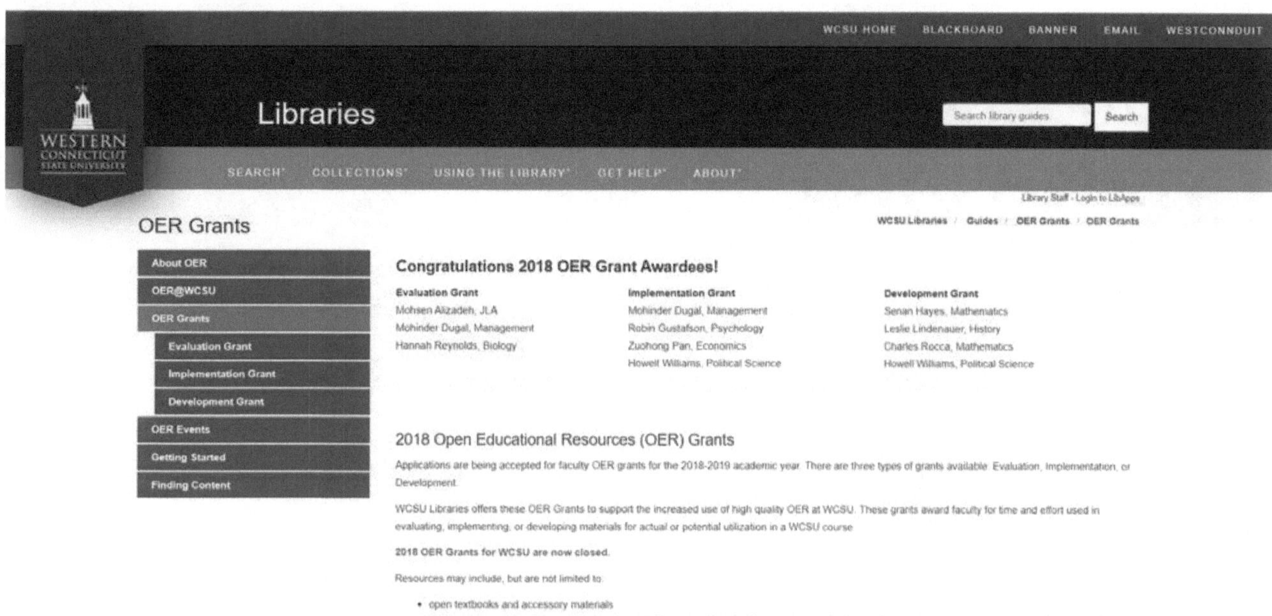

Western Connecticut State University offers three different grant opportunities. https://libguides.wcsu.edu/c.php?g=872002&p=6260049

OER INFORMATION

CONNECTICUT STATE COLLEGES AND UNIVERSITIES (CSCU)

Create OER

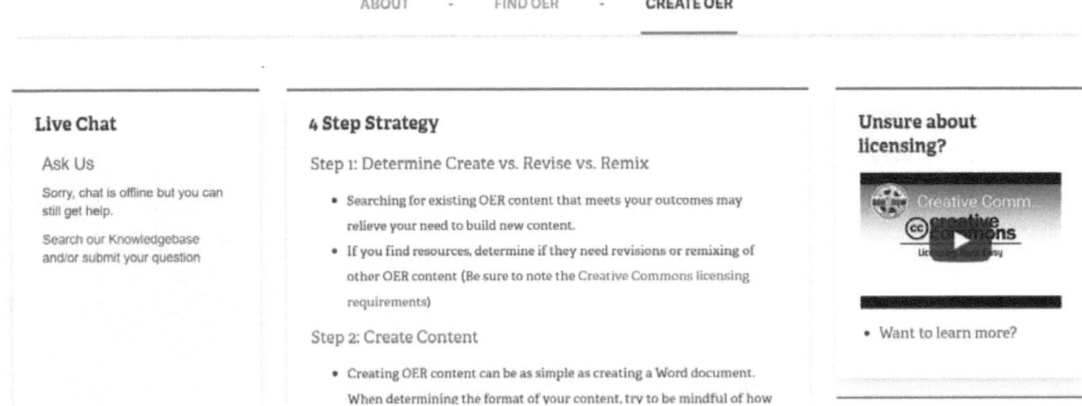

Connecticut State Colleges and Universities (CSCU) provide a brief overview of how to create OER. https://cscu.libguides.com/findoer/create

HOLLINS UNIVERSITY

OER Savings

OER SAVINGS (Spring 2016 - Spring 2020)

Professor	Class	Student Count	Savings
Gerber-Stroh	Film 334 Directing for Film	6	$210.00
	Film 373 Documentary Film & Televisi..	12	$300.00
Gettings	PHIL 120 Critical Thinking	8	$80.00
	PHIL 208 Feminist Philosophies	5	$175.00
	PHIL 223 Philosophy of Fiction	8	$80.00
Hernandez	ECON 157 Microeconomics	92	$1,564.00
Joseph	COMM 101	36	
Kennedy	MATH 140 Precalculus	36	$10,800.00
	MATH 241 Calculus 1	28	$8,400.00
	MATH 242 Calculus 2	2	$600.00
	Math 255 Methods of Matrices	10	$2,000.00
	MATH 316 Several Variable Calculus	9	$2,700.00
	MATH 351 Differential Equations	7	$1,400.00
Levering	MATH 241 Calculus 1	10	$3,000.00
	MATH 242 Calculus 2	5	$1,500.00
Lynch	MATH 242 Calculus 1	22	$6,600.00
Mann	PSY 141 Intro to Psych	17	$850.00
Messer-Bourgoin	BUS 100 Intro to Business	144	$7,200.00
Pempek	PSY 141 Intro to Psych	80	$11,200.00
Presswood	COMM290 - Critical Issues in Social M..	2	$96.00
	Digital Dining and Viral Media	27	$1,080.00
	Public Speaking	28	$868.00
Turner	GPS 214 Qualitative Methods	10	$500.00
Grand Total		**604**	**$61,203.00**

An interactive table laying out the savings to students with the OER program. http://library.hollins.edu/oer/

CC BY SA

SUSQUEHANNA UNIVERSITY

Open Educational Resources (OER): OER Myths

Susquehanna University has a webpage debunking OER myths. http://library.susqu.edu/c.php?g=908024&p=6586760

UNIVERSITY OF FINDLAY

Affordable Learning

Join librarians Drew Balduff and Andrew Whitis for a series of repeated one hour presentations in Shafer Library's Learning Commons to learn how you can save students money.

Introduction to Affordable Learning
Feb 18 at 10 am; Feb 28 at Noon; Mar 12 at 3:30 pm
What is it and why should you care? Why are we even talking about this?

Open Access and Open Educational Resources
Feb 19 at Noon; Feb 25 at 3:30 pm; Mar 14 at 10 am
What exactly are "open" resources and how can they be used in your course? Learn strategies for finding and evaluating open resources for course text adoption.

Library Licensed Content
Feb 20 at 3:30 pm; Feb 27 at 10 am; Mar 11 Noon
Did you know OhioLINK has been licensing digital scholarly content for 15 years? Learn how to find and incorporate library licensed online books and articles into your course.

Inclusive Access
Mar 19 at Noon; Mar 20 at 3:30 pm
OhioLINK has negotiated discounts with the major commercial textbook publishers. We will discuss the benefits and challenges of inclusive access.

University of Findlay's poster highlighting training sessions offered.

VALLEY CITY STATE UNIVERSITY

Faculty Looking to Implement OER

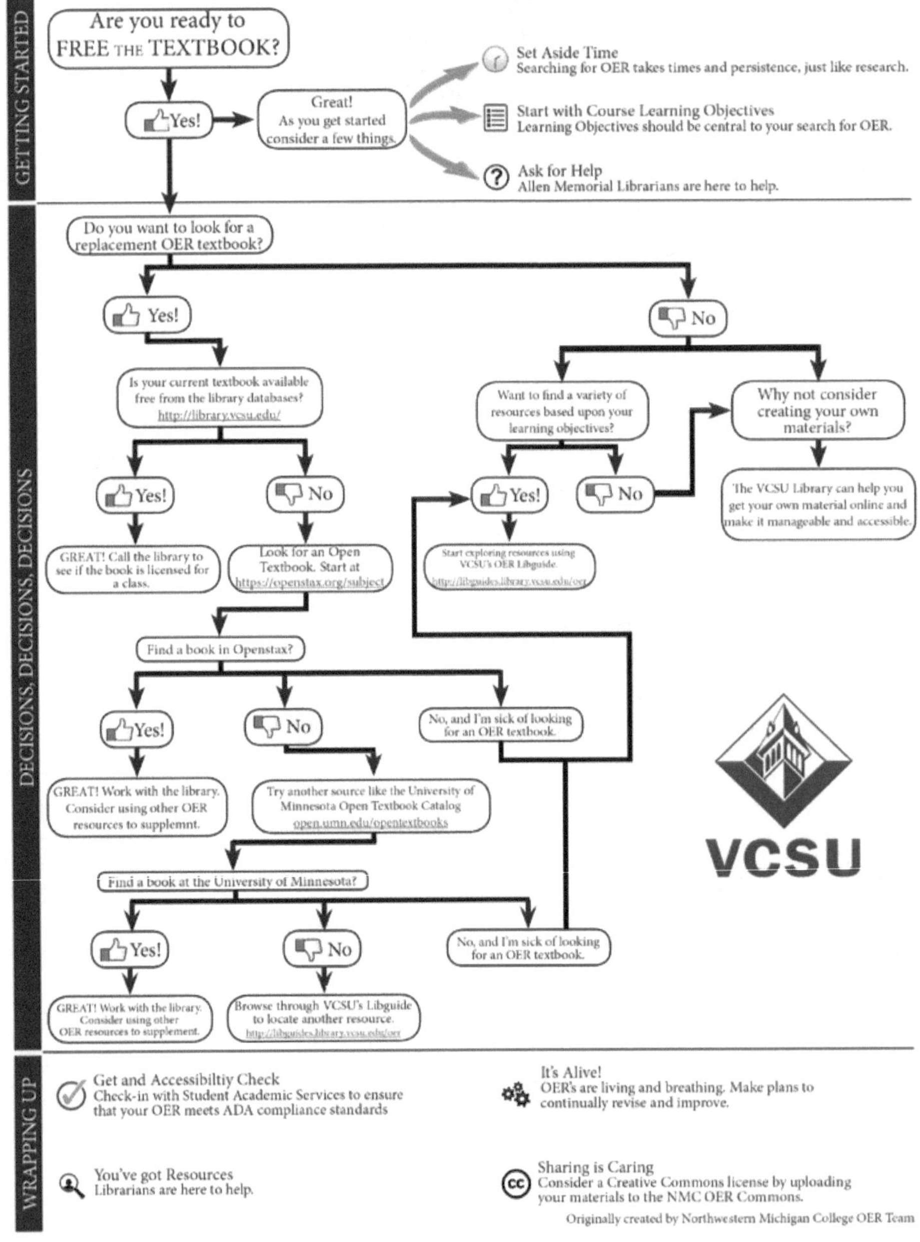

A flowchart for faculty looking to implement OER. http://www.vcsu.edu/cmsfiles/469/d4b63982bd.pdf?1562945406 [link no longer works]

WHEATON COLLEGE

Open Educational Resources

WALLACE LIBRARY

OPEN EDUCATIONAL RESOURCES

OEWHAT?

Open Educational Resources (OER) are teaching, learning, and research materials that reside in the public domain or have been released under a Creative Commons license. There are many low to no cost OER alternatives to traditional high priced textbooks.

THREE YEARS STRONG

The Wallace Library began support of OER on campus by hosting a workshop in 2015. Since then library staff have partnered with the Library, Technology, and Learning Committee to raise awareness of OER and fund stipends to faculty to utilize OER.

BIG SAVINGS

Since it began, Wheaton's OER initiative has saved students over $220,000 in textbook costs. This is an average of $162 per student in classes that used OER instead of traditional textbooks.

BIG BENEFITS

While OER is great for reducing the cost of higher education for students it has many other benefits. The flexibility of OER materials allows faculty to fully customize texts to class needs and learning outcomes.

KEY PARTNERS

Currently, OER materials are used in place of traditional textbooks in intro courses in Chemistry, Math, and Physics, as well as almost all Buisiness and Management Courses.

An institution-specific infographic describing OER for the campus. https://wheatoncollege.edu/academics/library/for-faculty/open-educational-resources/

OER PROGRAM DEVELOPMENT

DREW UNIVERSITY

Open Education Resources (OER) Task Force

OER Task Force 2019 draft

Beginning date: May 2019
End date: September 2019
Administrative Sponsors:
Andrew Bonamici, University Librarian *&/OR*
Debra Liebowitz, Provost
Members:
Library Administration: Andrew Bonamici (convener)
Instructional Tech: Nicole Pinto-Creazzo and Jenna Corraro
Library Reference & Instruction: Margery Ashmun; others?
Library Systems: Guy Dobson
Faculty Stakeholders/Participants: Jonathan Rose, John Lenz, and Sandra Keyser (all members of ULC)
THEO &/or CSGS rep(s): P. Kimberleigh Jordan
Also interested: Minjoon Kouh (who has already adopted OERs)
Student Government representative: Andrew is in touch with Vincent Costa about participating or finding another student rep

Background/Rationale

What are Open Educational Resources?

Open educational resources (OER) are teaching, learning, and research materials in any medium

that reside in the public domain or that have been released under an open license that permits no-cost access, use, adaptation, and redistribution by others. OER confer significant dollar savings while also giving learners ready access to a wide range of high-quality, highly flexible educational materials. Open content offers faculty a means to customize curriculum to better align with learner needs and interests and to collaborate in new ways with peers worldwide.

> "7 Things You Should Know About Open Education," EDUCAUSE Learning Initiative (2018). https://library.educause.edu/resources/2018/6/7-things-you-should-know-about-open-education-content

OER programs are required by statute in several states, now including New Jersey following passage of the Affordable College Textbook Act (S768_R1) in March 2019.

Recent Initiatives at Drew

The Drew Library and IT identified an OER initiative in the 2016–19 strategic plan as follows:

> II. Infuse the creative use of technological and digital services to expand the offerings of the Drew Libraries

> E. Intensify Library and IT support for use of reputable Open Educational Resources and Library resources in courses as substitutes for required reading texts (Ongoing)

In 2018–2019, the VALE NJ academic library consortium joined the Open Textbook Network, providing access to expert training and implementation resources.

Charge

The task force will:

- Identify current library and campus OER and affordable course content activities. (For example: current OER LibGuide)
- Recommend characteristics of courses where OER adoption would have high impact and likelihood of success (for example, high enrollment lower division gateway courses in disciplines with high textbook costs)
- Identify sources of support for instructors in discovery, curation, and adoption of OERs
- Recommend service and support models for a sustainable OER program

In addition to fully open OERs and textbooks, the task force may identify additional strategies to reduce or avoid costs to students; for example, using the Moodle LMS or other authenticated platforms to deliver materials already licensed by the Drew Library.

Deliverables

A report for review by Library Council, the University Library Committee, and the Provost, with contents including but not limited to:

- Summary of current OER services and affordable course content activities in the Drew library and on campus
- Examples of OER programs and service models in other institutions, including other NJ and Oberlin Group libraries (see 2018 Oberlin survey below)
- Existing institutional barriers and challenges to adoption
- Potential incentives for adoption
- Potential sources for incentives
- Recommendations for implementation, including
    - ✧ General scope, scale, and resource requirements of a campus OER and textbook cost-reduction initiative
    - ✧ Roles and responsibilities (e.g., library, inst tech, faculty, bookstore, others?)
    - ✧ Timeline, including phasing (for example, identifying "low hanging fruit" such as existing OERs that can be adopted as-is or with minimal revision, vs. creation of new works)
    - ✧ Faculty and staff training needs
    - ✧ Suggested avenues for campus outreach, marketing, and communications
    - ✧ Recurring cost/benefit for membership in OER consortia &/or advocacy organizations *[currently available through VALE participation in Open Textbook Network]*
    - ✧ Assessment and reporting (for example, preparation and submission of Drew's OER plan to the NJ Secretary of Higher Education, per S.768)

Task Force Timeline

- April–May 2019: Appoint Task Force
- May 2019: Kick-off convening for all participants; review charge and timeline
- Summer 2019: Inst Tech/Library workshop(s) and consultations with faculty stakeholders/participants, with goal of identifying one or more OER/cost reduction strategies for adoption during AY2019–20
- Fall 2019: report with recommendations; summary report of experience to date
- *N.B.: this will conclude summer task force charge; however, faculty participants will be supported in their OER efforts as needed through AY2019–20.*

Resource People or Teams

- General Oversight (Policies, Legal, Compliance, Licensing): University Librarian, Library Council, ULC, University legal representatives, (Bookstore?), others TBD
- Pedagogy: ITS (instructional design), Center for Academic Excellence, reference and instruction librarians, other student success partners TBD

- Technical (Design, Production, Storage, Delivery): Library Systems, ITS, UTS, others TBD
- Training, Faculty Development: ITS, subject librarians, CAE, others TBD
- Marketing, Outreach: web and social media teams, subject librarians, faculty adopters, students, others TBD

Reference

Other Libraries

Claybaugh, Z., & Stone, C. (2017). *Open educational resource 2017 textbook list.* Fairfield, CT: Sacred Heart University. Retrieved from http://digitalcommons.sacredheart.edu/cgi/viewcontent.cgi?article=1047&context=library_staff (retrieved September 12, 2017)

SPARC Library OER Forum. Retrieved from https://groups.google.com/a/sparcopen.org/forum/#!forum/liboer

VALE OER Task Force and consortial membership in Open Textbook Network (see below from Megan Dempsey).

Walz, A., Jensen, K., and Salem, J. A., Jr. (2016). *Affordable course content and open educational resources. SPEC Kit 351.* Washington, DC: Association of Research Libraries. https://doi.org/10.29242/spec.351

Other Higher Education

- EDUCAUSE Seven Things 3-part series (2018): https://library.educause.edu/resources/2018/7/7-things-you-should-know-about-open-education-practices
- EDUCAUSE Library | Open Educational Resources (OER): https://library.educause.edu/topics/teaching-and-learning/open-educational-resources-oer
- OpenStax:_https://open.umn.edu/opentextbooks/
- Open Textbook Network: https://research.cehd.umn.edu/otn/)n
- Merlot II: https://www.merlot.org/merlot/index.htm

Federal Policy initiatives

- Affordable College Textbook Act Reintroduced again in 116th Congress: https://sparcopen.org/wp-content/uploads/2019/04/20190404_Affordable_College_Textbook_Act.pdf

FORT HAYS STATE UNIVERSITY

Grant Proposal Summary with Funding Structure

FHSU Z-Course Grant Proposal Summary

Brief Overview

A Z-Course is a course which requires zero-cost to students for the purchase of course materials such as textbooks, coursepacks, subscriptions, or homework. The goals of the FHSU Z-Course Grant Proposal are:

1. To reduce the cost of education for students enrolling in Z-Courses by eliminating the need to purchase textbooks or course materials.
2. To incentivize departments with large-enrollment courses to develop or adopt free alternatives to traditional print textbooks and course materials.

The Z-Course proposal is funded by charging FHSU students enrolling in a Z-Course a minimal cost in lieu of requiring them to purchase commercial textbooks or course material costs. The cost-share will support grants to faculty to develop or adopt zero-cost materials, costs for maintaining the program, and operational funds to departments as an incentive to participate.

Students win because course costs are dramatically reduced. The College Board estimated that the national average cost per course for textbooks and course materials is $153.*

Faculty win because they receive grant funding to convert their traditional course requiring students to purchase commercial textbooks and materials to Z-Courses.

Departments win because the more course sections that are converted to Z-Courses, the more funding the department receives to meet needs.

* https://uspirg.org/reports/usp/open-101

Funding Model

A $12 course student cost-share is charged for any Z-Course. Based on national data a student would save an average of $141 per course. Only students enrolling in a Z-Course pay the cost-share.

$6 of the student cost-share goes to the faculty member's department each semester that the course is offered for enrollment as a Z-Course. If a course reverts to use of commercial course materials, students no longer pay the cost-share and the department no longer receives Z-Course funds for that course. Existing courses that can certify that they are zero-cost will be eligible to receive the cost-share.

$6 of the student cost-share goes to the OER program to provide grants to faculty for Z-Course development and for tools and training necessary to support Z-Course development.

The grants program will favor large multi-section courses enrolling at least 500 students annually. A 500 student Z-Course with a $12/student will provide $6,000 per year in revenue. Half of that amount will be used for Z-Course faculty grants, software, training, or other direct operational costs to necessary develop and maintain the program.

FHSU Z-Course Grant Full Proposal

Introduction

The purpose of the Z-Course Grant is to incentivize departments with large-enrollment courses to convert courses so that students are not required to purchase any course materials. Seed funding for this grant is provided through the Foundation funding. Students taking courses that use zero-cost course materials will be charged a $12 Z-Course cost-share in lieu of traditional course material costs. $6 of this cost-share will go to the department to incentivize conversion and support ongoing updates and maintenance of z-courses. The department may spend this funding as needed for operational costs. The other $6 will go back to the OER program to pay for faculty grants, technology and training, or other direct program expenses.

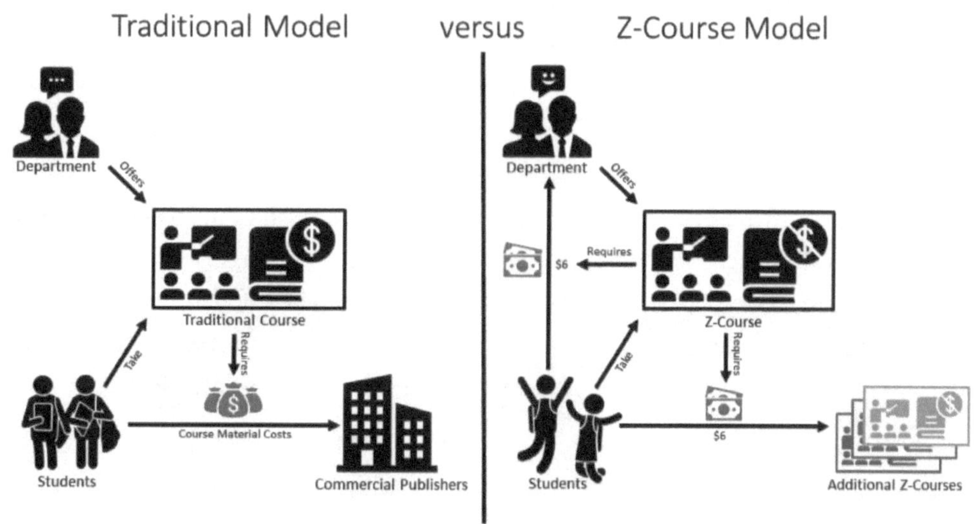

Icons CC BY The Noun Project: "Communication" & "Couple," Gregor Cresnar; "Class," Rflor; "dollar book" and "dollar block book," Vectorstall PK; "University Students" & "Jumping Students," ProSymbols; "money bags," Sergey Demushkin RU; "company," Rose Alice design; "Money," sandiindra ID

Funding

Seed funding for this grant is provided by Foundation funding with a goal for the Z-Course Program is become self-sustaining through a Z-Course cost-share. Students enrolling in Z-Courses that use only zero-cost course materials would incur a $12 per course cost-share in lieu of buying traditional course material. $6 of this cost-share will go to the department to incentivize conversion and support ongoing updates and maintenance of Z-Courses. The department may spend this funding as needed for its internal operational costs. The other $6 will go back to the zero-course-material-cost fund to fund faculty Z-Course grants, technology and training, or other direct program costs.

Methods

Course materials include textbooks, course packs, readings, lab manuals, homework systems, and other supplementary content. Note that this definition does not include physical lab materials or software. Course materials may be replaced in several ways:

- With open educational resources (OERs), such as open textbooks. OERs are course materials that are free and available under an open license. At a minimum, an open license allows users to make and distribute copies of the resource, activities that are not usually permitted under copyright law. Open textbooks are openly licensed books providing an overview of existing knowledge for the purposes of systematic learning.
- With free but traditionally copyrighted resources, such as professional websites; and/or
- With existing library-licensed materials, such as e-books or articles.

Instructors may choose to use existing materials, adapt existing materials (copyright permitting), or author new materials. Any new materials authored must be placed under an open license that permits free copying, redistribution, and editing.

Eligibility

Courses submitted for the Z-Course Grant must meet the following requirements:

- Our priority is the conversion of large-enrollment and general-education courses. Therefore, preference will be given to applications to convert courses with an annual enrollment of at least 500 students, particularly if all faculty who teach sections of the course have agreed to switch to zero-cost course materials.
- The course must require textual course materials that could be replaced. Practica, exercise classes, etc. are not eligible unless they require textual course materials.
- At the time of application, there must be a cost for course materials. Courses that already have zero course material cost (z-courses) are not eligible. However, departments may request that the Z-Course cost-share be applied to existing Z-Courses and Z-Sections.
- Examples are provided in Appendix A.

Conversion Process

Grant recipients will participate in a one-week "course conversion boot camp" with a cohort of other Z-Course faculty. The boot camp will begin on the Tuesday after final grades are due for the spring semester. A team of librarians and instructional designers will be on hand to provide information about best practices; assist with finding, adapting, and/or authoring course materials; and answer questions. Participants will then have twelve weeks over the summer to finish converting the course, with the goal of implementing changes in the fall semester. Half of the course conversion stipend will be paid to the participant(s) at the end of the boot camp, and half when the conversion is complete. If there are multiple participants collaborating on the same course, the stipend will be divided between them. The department will receive Z-Course cost-share funding starting in the first semester when the course is offered at zero course material cost.

How to Apply

The applicant(s) will make a presentation to the OER Committee explaining their proposal for the course to be converted. The presentation should be no longer than 30 minutes, including time for questions. The applicant(s) should provide the following information in their presentation:

- The name and number of the course
- The approximate annual enrollment for the sections of the course that will be converted (do not count sections that will continue to use paid resources)
- A description of the paid resource(s) to be replaced, including the title, publisher, and list price of any textbooks currently being used
- The amount of money that will be saved annually (approximate annual enrollment for sections to be converted, times money saved per student)
- A description of the work needed to convert the course—can it be converted using existing zero-cost resources, or will conversion require adapting or authoring materials?

Funding Structure

Seed funding for the Z-Course Grant comes from the FHSU Foundation. However, our goal is for the program to become self-sustaining. Therefore, we propose to charge a $12 Z-Course Cost-share to students who enroll in Z-Courses. This cost-share will take the place of existing course material costs. $6 of this cost-share will go to the department offering the course, and $6 will go back to the Z-Course program.

APPENDIX A: EXAMPLES

- HHP 103: Exercise through Housework does not use any textual course materials. The course is not eligible for the Z-Course Grant or the Z-course cost-share because it does not have textual course materials that can be replaced.
- TECS 121: Building Prototypes does not use a textbook, coursepack, or homework system, but the students pay a $50 materials cost-share for balsa wood, foam, glue, etc. The course is not eligible for the Z-Course Grant or the Z-Course cost-share because it does not have textual course materials that can be replaced.
- SOC 141: Learning from Fictional Cultures: There are two instructors who teach sections of SOC 141, Zuzen Archambault and Mihail Dixon. Dr. Archambault currently teaches using a library-licensed e-book called *Examining Imaginary Societies* ($0). However, Dr. Dixon teaches using a workbook called *Analyzing Cultural Elements of Literature* ($15). Dr. Archambault can request that his sections have the Z-Course cost-share applied to them.
- BCOM 211: Talking to Technical Experts: The instructors, Jacob Langbroek and Lashay Sommer, are both currently using an open textbook called *IT Basics for Businesspeople* ($0) and some readings from Forsyth Library ($0). Because the course already has zero course material cost, Mr. Langbroek and Ms. Sommer cannot apply for the Z-Course Grant. However, they request that the Z-Course cost-share be applied to the course because it has zero course material cost.
- MUS 124: Beginning Harp currently uses the textbook *Harmonious Harping* ($150). One of the instructors, Wendy Brankovic, has found a number of free online resources related to playing the harp and would like to convert the course to have zero course material cost. She approaches the other faculty members who teach sections of MUS 124, Maury O'Callaghan and Kirabo Boveri, as well as the department chair, about applying for the Z-Course Grant. However, Dr. O'Callaghan and Dr. Boveri say that they would prefer to continue using *Harmonious Harping*. Dr. Brankovic applies for the Z-Course Grant on her own and must calculate the potential savings using the annual enrollment for only the sections she teaches.
- NURS 105: Team-Based Care currently uses a $35 coursepack. One of the instructors, Janine Pedersen, is eager to convert the course to have zero course material cost. She talks to the other two faculty members who teach sections of NURS 105, Sylvana Rinne and Gaspard Pawlitzki, and they all agree to offer the course with zero course material cost. Since Dr. Rinne and Dr. Pawlitzki don't feel the need to be involved in the course conversion process, Dr. Pedersen applies for the Z-Course Grant on her own. She can calculate the potential savings using the annual enrollment from all sections. Dr. Pedersen participates in the course conversion boot camp and finishes converting the course, receiving the course conversion stipend. In the fall, Dr. Pedersen, Dr. Rinne, and Dr. Pawlitzki all teach the course at zero course material cost and the Z-Course cost-share is applied to NURS 105.
- TEEL 203: Preparing the Classroom: Currently, all of the instructors for the course are

using different commercially published textbooks. However, at a departmental meeting, the department chair brings up the possibility of converting TEEL 203 to use zero-cost course materials. All of the faculty members teaching sections of the course agree, and they choose Mr. Efraim Anson and Dr. Nandita Macek to serve as the lead developers. Mr. Anson and Dr. Macek apply for the Z-Course Grant together, counting the total annual enrollment for all course sections. Mr. Anson and Dr. Macek both participate in the course conversion boot camp and collaborate to finish converting the course, splitting the course conversion stipend. In the fall, the instructors for all sections teach TEEL 203 at zero course material cost and the Z-Course cost-share is applied.

FURMAN UNIVERSITY

OER Review Program Overview

Summary

In summer of 2016, Furman University, Duke University, Davidson College, and Johnson C. Smith University received funding from The Duke Endowment Libraries to launch an Open Educational Resources (OER) Review Program at their respective institutions. The program serves to educate instructors at the four Duke Endowed campuses in the identification and assessment of OER thereby creating an opportunity for them to gain familiarity with open learning objects before committing to adoption.

Background

A recent study found that college textbook costs have increased a staggering 945% between 1978 and 2014 (Perry, 2015). Moreover, research indicates that if students cannot afford course materials, 65% of them will avoid renting or buying texts even though they know it may possibly impact their overall success in the course (Senack, 2014).

Open Educational Resources (OER) offer a solution to this problem. OER are teaching and learning materials that are freely available online with few use restrictions. Examples of OER include textbooks, tutorials, videos, and lectures. A study at Virginia State University found that students who took courses that utilized OER materials "tended to have higher grades and lower failing and withdrawal rates" (Feldstein et al., 2012, "Student outcomes with digital textbooks," para. 3). Additionally, Wiley (2013) argues that involving students in the adaptation and re-sharing of OER can make learning more public and meaningful for students.

Despite the many benefits of using OER materials, there is still a huge knowledge gap when it comes to understanding and adopting these resources. Faculty may not be aware of the resources available to them or how to determine which materials are the best fit for their classes. The libraries at Furman University, Davidson College, Johnson C. Smith University, and Duke University are attempting to bridge this gap by conducting an OER Review Program at each of their individual institutions.

Program Overview

The program has two core components: an internal education program for participating libraries and the faculty review program.

In order to facilitate awareness of OERs on their respective campuses, two librarians from each institution attended Train the Trainer session on OERs in July 2016. This one-day workshop was led by Will Cross, Director of the Copyright & Digital Scholarship Center at the North Carolina State University Libraries. Mr. Cross educated the librarians on the benefits and drawbacks of OERs; understanding campus climate; and the nuts-and-bolts of locating, evaluating, and implementing OERs. He also facilitated important discussions of purpose and implementation of this particular program on the four campuses.

Having gained a better internal understanding of OERs, the librarians now lead a faculty review program on each campus for the academic year. While there is some standardization of language and form across all four campuses, the collaborators agreed to leave details of program execution up to individual institutions so that each could be tailored to meet the needs and resources of their stakeholders. At Furman University, the following protocol has been put into place:

1. Furman faculty express interest in the program by filling out an interest form available here: http://libguides.furman.edu/oer-review. The number of Furman participants is capped at 10.
2. Participants are selected by Furman librarians Andrea Wright (Science Librarian and University Copyright Officer) and Christy Allen (Assistant Director for Discovery Services). The selection criteria include: perceived level of engagement, variety among disciplines, and enrollment size of class.
3. Participants attend a one-hour workshop on OER presented by Andrea and/or Christy. The workshop begins with an overview of the program. A brief presentation on OER licensing, evaluation, and discovery is followed by time for the participants to work with a librarian to identify appropriate existing OER based on their class or topic needs.
4. Participants review the OER that they selected. This can be 1 OER textbook or a compilation of 2–3 smaller resources such as tutorials, assessments, lectures, or class activities.
5. Participants will complete a written review for each selected OER using a standardized form based on the BC Open Textbooks Review Criteria (BCcampus, n.d.). Faculty will submit the forms to the librarian at their institution.
6. Each participant who completes all steps of the program will be awarded a $250 stipend.
7. A follow-up survey will be sent to participants in summer 2017 to assess the training session, as well as their knowledge and application of OER concepts, OER identification, the review process, and potential OER adoption.
8. The results collected during the program will be analyzed at the institution level and also aggregated with results from all the participating Duke Endowed partners. Anticipated analyses include: efficacy of OER in comparison to traditional learning objects; interest in OER adoption among program participants; identification of common themes, benefits, challenges, and trends among reviews; and identification of future OER initiatives supported by the libraries.

Current Status

The program was briefly pitched at the start of the semester at the New Faculty Library Orientation and the Undergraduate Evening Studies Faculty Orientation. With just those two events as marketing, as of September 2016, at Furman University:

- 8 faculty have expressed interest in participating in the OER program.
- 6 of these faculty have attended an OER workshop taught by Andrea and Christy, and the remaining 2 are scheduled for workshops in October.
- 2 of these faculty have completed consent forms and are official participants in the program.
- Andrea and Christy will continue to market this program to faculty and anticipate filling all 10 available slots.

The larger TDEL collaboration is scheduled to have a group conference call mid-fall to compare responses and discuss questions or concerns as the program continues into spring.

Online Resources

- Furman Libraries' OER website: http://libguides.furman.edu/oer
- OER Review Program website: http://libguides.furman.edu/oer-review

Bibliography

BCcampus. (n.d.). BC open textbooks review criteria. Retrieved from https://open.bccampus.ca/bc-open-textbooks-review-criteria/

Feldstein, A., Martin, M., Hudson, A., Warren, K., Hilton, J., & Wiley, D. (2012). Open textbooks and increased student access and outcomes. *European Journal of Open, Distance and E-Learning, 2.* Retrieved from https://files.eric.ed.gov/fulltext/EJ992490.pdf

Perry, M. J. (2015). The new era of the $400 college textbook, which is part of the unsustainable higher education bubble. [Blog post]. Retrieved from https://www.aei.org/publication/the-new-era-of-the-400-college-textbook-which-is-part-of-the-unsustainable-higher-education-bubble/

Senack, E. (2014). *Fixing the broken textbook market: How students respond to high textbook costs and demand alternatives.* U.S. PIRG Education Fund and the Student PIRGs. Retrieved from http://www.uspirg.org/reports/usp/fixing-broken-textbook-market

Wiley, D. (2013, October 21). What is open pedagogy? [Blog post]. Retrieved from http://opencontent.org/blog/archives/2975

SAINT XAVIER UNIVERSITY

Open Educational Resources

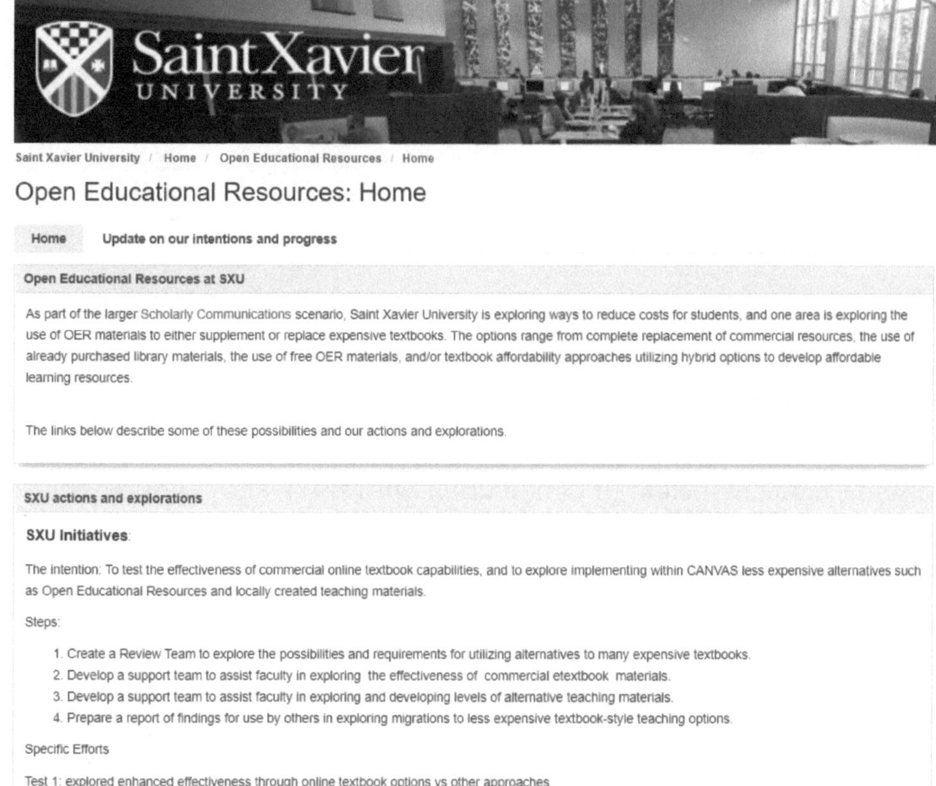

Saint Xavier University / Home / Open Educational Resources / Home

Open Educational Resources: Home

Home | Update on our intentions and progress

Open Educational Resources at SXU

As part of the larger Scholarly Communications scenario, Saint Xavier University is exploring ways to reduce costs for students, and one area is exploring the use of OER materials to either supplement or replace expensive textbooks. The options range from complete replacement of commercial resources, the use of already purchased library materials, the use of free OER materials, and/or textbook affordability approaches utilizing hybrid options to develop affordable learning resources.

The links below describe some of these possibilities and our actions and explorations.

SXU actions and explorations

SXU Initiatives:

The intention: To test the effectiveness of commercial online textbook capabilities, and to explore implementing within CANVAS less expensive alternatives such as Open Educational Resources and locally created teaching materials.

Steps:

1. Create a Review Team to explore the possibilities and requirements for utilizing alternatives to many expensive textbooks.
2. Develop a support team to assist faculty in exploring the effectiveness of commercial etextbook materials.
3. Develop a support team to assist faculty in exploring and developing levels of alternative teaching materials.
4. Prepare a report of findings for use by others in exploring migrations to less expensive textbook-style teaching options.

Specific Efforts

Test 1: explored enhanced effectiveness through online textbook options vs other approaches

Saint Xavier University describes their early state planning for OER. https://lib.sxu.edu/oer/OERefforts

STATE UNIVERSITY OF NEW YORK (SUNY)

OER Sustainability Planning Guide and Template

Institution Name: ______________________________ Date: __________
Contact Name: ______________________________ Email: __________________

SUNY institutions receiving System funding to support the adoption and expansion of Open Education Resources (OER) are required to submit a sustainability plan as a condition of participation. Use the planning template below in conjunction with the Field Guide to assist in developing a sustainability plan for your campus.

The SUNY System Office will provide institutions with a link to an online survey form to submit the necessary information to satisfy the sustainability plan requirement.

Adoption Rating Scale
0 = No activity is underway.
1 = Planning—An approach to the activity is designed and/or meeting organization and preparation is underway.
2 = Developing—Substantive work is underway to complete the activity.
3 = Operational—Initial outcomes/implementation/products are available for the activity.
4 = Accomplished/ongoing—Final implementation/draft/action for the activity is complete, or final processes/plan is in place for continuation of the activity.

OER Sustainability Planning Activities: Infrastructure	Status of Current Adoption (Rating Scale Definitions Shown at End of Template)	Progress to Date Implementing Activity
1. Guidelines a. Develop OER Guidelines that provide guidance on: • OER objectives and course expectations, • OER course development procedures and requirements, • Available PD and technical support, • OER course review and approval process.	❒ No activity (0) ❒ Planning (1) ❒ Developing (2) ❒ Operational (3) ❒ Accomplished/Ongoing (4)	Progress to date:

OER Sustainability Planning Activities: Infrastructure	Status of Current Adoption (Rating Scale Definitions Shown at End of Template)	Progress to Date Implementing Activity
2. Processes a. Establish process for proposing OER courses/sections, including development of proposal forms; evaluation rubrics, and tools for administrative oversight.	❒ No activity (0) ❒ Planning (1) ❒ Developing (2) ❒ Operational (3) ❒ Accomplished/Ongoing (4)	Progress to date:
b. Establish process for OER course review and approval, including evaluation criteria/rubrics.	❒ No activity (0) ❒ Planning (1) ❒ Developing (2) ❒ Operational (3) ❒ Accomplished/Ongoing (4)	Progress to date:
c. Identify the stipend/incentive policy in place at the institution, including any framework for differentiated stipends; payment schedule; course conversion requirements, and timeframe for providing financial incentives.	❒ No activity (0) ❒ Planning (1) ❒ Developing (2) ❒ Operational (3) ❒ Accomplished/Ongoing (4)	Progress to date:
3. Professional Development and Support a. Identify/develop ongoing professional development opportunities for faculty, including communication strategy for accessing those resources (e.g., library; workshops; faculty champions).	❒ No activity (0) ❒ Planning (1) ❒ Developing (2) ❒ Operational (3) ❒ Accomplished/Ongoing (4)	Progress to date:
b. Identify/develop ongoing supports that IT/ID can provide and the procedures faculty should follow to access those supports (e.g., design support; loading online OER resources into the LMS).	❒ No activity (0) ❒ Planning (1) ❒ Developing (2) ❒ Operational (3) ❒ Accomplished/Ongoing (4)	Progress to date:
4. Platforms a. Implement technology to identify OER courses in ERP systems; develop a process for identifying and reporting OER courses in those systems.	❒ No activity (0) ❒ Planning (1) ❒ Developing (2) ❒ Operational (3) ❒ Accomplished/Ongoing (4)	Progress to date:
b. Add an OER identifier to the course catalogue that allows students to search for OER courses.	❒ No activity (0) ❒ Planning (1) ❒ Developing (2) ❒ Operational (3) ❒ Accomplished/Ongoing (4)	Progress to date:

OER Sustainability Planning Activities: Infrastructure	Status of Current Adoption (Rating Scale Definitions Shown at End of Template)	Progress to Date Implementing Activity
c. Identify/develop process by which faculty can integrate their online OER course materials into the LMS.	❒ No activity (0) ❒ Planning (1) ❒ Developing (2) ❒ Operational (3) ❒ Accomplished/Ongoing (4)	Progress to date:
d. Determine what platforms allow faculty to share the OER courses/course materials they developed.	❒ No activity (0) ❒ Planning (1) ❒ Developing (2) ❒ Operational (3) ❒ Accomplished/Ongoing (4)	Progress to date:
e. Determine what platforms/ procedures the bookstore and/ or print shop can offer students in OER courses (e.g., identify OER sections; offer low-cost print materials; ability to directly process an OER course fee).	❒ No activity (0) ❒ Planning (1) ❒ Developing (2) ❒ Operational (3) ❒ Accomplished/Ongoing (4)	Progress to date:
5. People and Organizational Framework a. Plan how a mature OER program will operate, including the organizational structure, leadership, and staffing requirements.	❒ No activity (0) ❒ Planning (1) ❒ Developing (2) ❒ Operational (3) ❒ Accomplished/Ongoing (4)	Progress to date:
b. Identify the interim supports necessary while transitioning towards the mature vision of OER.	❒ No activity (0) ❒ Planning (1) ❒ Developing (2) ❒ Operational (3) ❒ Accomplished/Ongoing (4)	Progress to date:
c. Identify new staff, or reallocated time of existing staff, required to sustain the OER model envisioned.	❒ No activity (0) ❒ Planning (1) ❒ Developing (2) ❒ Operational (3) ❒ Accomplished/Ongoing (4)	Progress to date:
d. Consider how OER could be infused into job descriptions, hiring requirements, and/ or tenure and promotion guidelines.	❒ No activity (0) ❒ Planning (1) ❒ Developing (2) ❒ Operational (3) ❒ Accomplished/Ongoing (4)	Progress to date:
6. Other (please describe)	❒ No activity (0) ❒ Planning (1) ❒ Developing (2) ❒ Operational (3) ❒ Accomplished/Ongoing (4)	Progress to date:

OER Sustainability Planning Activities: Resources	Status of Current Adoption (Rating Scale Definitions Shown at End of Template)	Progress to Date Implementing Activity
1. Finances a. Prepare a multi-year budget estimate for OER, including resources required for transitional and mature OER models (include new/reallocated staff time, stipends, PD, communication activities, etc.)	❒ No activity (0) ❒ Planning (1) ❒ Developing (2) ❒ Operational (3) ❒ Accomplished/Ongoing (4)	Progress to date:
b. Estimate the impact of OER on student success (DFW rates; persistence/retention) and the potential financial implications for students and the institution (e.g., tuition recapture).	❒ No activity (0) ❒ Planning (1) ❒ Developing (2) ❒ Operational (3) ❒ Accomplished/Ongoing (4)	Progress to date:
c. Determine whether an OER fee will be proposed; its specifications and the approval process required.	❒ No activity (0) ❒ Planning (1) ❒ Developing (2) ❒ Operational (3) ❒ Accomplished/Ongoing (4)	Progress to date:
d. Estimate the financial impact of OER on the bookstore and the commission/profit transferred to the university/college.	❒ No activity (0) ❒ Planning (1) ❒ Developing (2) ❒ Operational (3) ❒ Accomplished/Ongoing (4)	Progress to date:
2. Efficiency a. Review/revise existing OER policies and procedures to generate programmatic efficiencies (e.g., incentivize high-cost/high-enrollment course conversions; promote common OER courses).	❒ No activity (0) ❒ Planning (1) ❒ Developing (2) ❒ Operational (3) ❒ Accomplished/Ongoing (4)	Progress to date:
b. Coordinate with support units and determine how their services can be leveraged to support OER.	❒ No activity (0) ❒ Planning (1) ❒ Developing (2) ❒ Operational (3) ❒ Accomplished/Ongoing (4)	Progress to date:
3. Other (please describe)	❒ No activity (0) ❒ Planning (1) ❒ Developing (2) ❒ Operational (3) ❒ Accomplished/Ongoing (4)	Progress to date:

OER Sustainability Planning Activities: Culture	Status of Current Adoption (Rating Scale Definitions Shown at End of Template)	Progress to Date Implementing Activity
1. Vision and Strategy a. Detail how OER supports the college's strategic vision/goals/plan.	❒ No activity (0) ❒ Planning (1) ❒ Developing (2) ❒ Operational (3) ❒ Accomplished/Ongoing (4)	Progress to date:
b. Meet with college leadership to discuss OER activity and connections to strategic vision/goal/plan; seek leadership on promoting an OER culture on campus.	❒ No activity (0) ❒ Planning (1) ❒ Developing (2) ❒ Operational (3) ❒ Accomplished/Ongoing (4)	Progress to date:
2. Metrics a. Report to academic deans/VP and SUNY System on number of OER courses, sections, and student enrollments each term.	❒ No activity (0) ❒ Planning (1) ❒ Developing (2) ❒ Operational (3) ❒ Accomplished/Ongoing (4)	Progress to date:
b. Estimate and report student savings from reduced textbook purchases; consider adjustments for student purchasing patterns and OER material costs.	❒ No activity (0) ❒ Planning (1) ❒ Developing (2) ❒ Operational (3) ❒ Accomplished/Ongoing (4)	Progress to date:
c. Partner with IR staff to examine impact of OER on student success (DFW rates; persistence/retention) and estimate the financial impact of those changes on students and the institution.	❒ No activity (0) ❒ Planning (1) ❒ Developing (2) ❒ Operational (3) ❒ Accomplished/Ongoing (4)	Progress to date:
d. Conduct periodic review of OER outcomes, successes, and challenges and indicate the process for addressing challenges that may arise.	❒ No activity (0) ❒ Planning (1) ❒ Developing (2) ❒ Operational (3) ❒ Accomplished/Ongoing (4)	Progress to date:
3. Communication a. Develop communication materials to inform faculty about OER and its impacts using multiple communication vehicles.	❒ No activity (0) ❒ Planning (1) ❒ Developing (2) ❒ Operational (3) ❒ Accomplished/Ongoing (4)	Progress to date:
b. Launch communication campaign to educate students about OER and how to identify OER courses.	❒ No activity (0) ❒ Planning (1) ❒ Developing (2) ❒ Operational (3) ❒ Accomplished/Ongoing (4)	Progress to date:

OER Sustainability Planning Activities: Culture	Status of Current Adoption (Rating Scale Definitions Shown at End of Template)	Progress to Date Implementing Activity
c. Educate administrators about OER activities, successes, and connection to broader campus goals using multiple communication vehicles.	❒ No activity (0) ❒ Planning (1) ❒ Developing (2) ❒ Operational (3) ❒ Accomplished/Ongoing (4)	Progress to date:
4. Other (please describe)	❒ No activity (0) ❒ Planning (1) ❒ Developing (2) ❒ Operational (3) ❒ Accomplished/Ongoing (4)	Progress to date:

Please answer the following questions:

1. Describe the sustainability elements your college/university will prioritize over the next year (if those priorities are still undetermined, please respond accordingly).

2. Identify those areas of the sustainability framework that will present the greatest challenges and describe why.

Developed by rpk GROUP, November 2018
Reporting framework adapted from:
Community College Research Center. (2017, June). *Guided pathways essential practices: Scale of adoption self-assessment*. New York: Teacher's College, Columbia University (June). https://ccrc.tc.columbia.edu/publications/what-we-know-about-guided-pathways-packet.html